BOWLING eXecution

John Jowdy

Human Kinetics

Library of Congress Cataloging-in-Publication Data

Jowdy, John, 1920-
  Bowling execution / John Jowdy
      p. cm.
Includes index.
  ISBN 0-7360-4217-2
 1. Bowling. I. Title.
  GV903.J69 2002
  794.6--dc21

2002020869

ISBN: 0-7360-4217-2

Acquisitions Editor: Ed McNeely; **Developmental Editor:** Laura Hambly; **Assistant Editors:** Dan Brachtesende and Kim Thoren; **Copyeditor:** Jan Feeney; **Proofreader:** Susan C. Hagan; **Indexer:** Betty Frizzéll; **Graphic Designer:** Robert Reuther; **Graphic Artist:** Tara Welsch; **Cover Designer:** Keith Blomberg; **Photo Manager:** Les Woodrum; **Photographer (cover):** Tom Roberts; **Cover Model:** Brian Voss; **Photographer (interior):** Tom Roberts and Les Woodrum, unless otherwise noted; **Art Manager:** Carl Johnson; **Illustrator:** Roberto Sabas; **Printer:** United Graphics

Human Kinetics books are available at special discounts for bulk purchase. Special editions or book excerpts can also be created to specification. For details, contact the Special Sales Manager at Human Kinetics.

Printed in the United States of America   10 9 8 7 6 5 4 3

Human Kinetics
Web site: www.HumanKinetics.com

United States: Human Kinetics, P.O. Box 5076, Champaign, IL 61825-5076
800-747-4457
e-mail: humank@hkusa.com

Canada: Human Kinetics, 475 Devonshire Road, Unit 100, Windsor, ON N8Y 2L5
800-465-7301 (in Canada only)
e-mail: orders@hkcanada.com

Europe: Human Kinetics, 107 Bradford Road, Stanningley
Leeds LS28 6AT, United Kingdom
+44 (0) 113 255 5665
e-mail: hk@hkeurope.com

Australia: Human Kinetics, 57A Price Avenue, Lower Mitcham, South Australia 5062
08 8277 1555
e-mail: liahka@senet.com.au

New Zealand: Human Kinetics, P.O. Box 105-231, Auckland Central
09-523-3462
e-mail: hkp@ihug.co.nz

I dedicate this book to my wife, Brenda: my best friend, my editor, my inspiration, and the love of my life. She contributed as much as, if not more than, I did to making this book a reality. Her contributions were invaluable.

Contents

Foreword

I'm not much of a writer; I am a fair bowler and top-notch fisherman. Ordinarily, when I start to write something, my mind goes blank. But as I started to write this foreword for John Jowdy's book, every word simply flowed out. I believe this writing came so easily for me because it is simply the truth.

Talent can be measured in many ways. The abilities to shoot a basketball from 30 feet with consistent accuracy, to drive a racecar at speeds beyond human imagination, and to throw a bowling ball at a target with flawless repetition are gifts from God. In most cases, these talents are deep within us, and we wander around aimlessly until they are extracted. The ability for someone to extract that talent is a gift in itself.

For the first seven years of my professional bowling career, I walked blindly through the corridors of not knowing why I wasn't performing to my potential. I settled for mediocrity in the struggle to make a living at bowling.

I have always known that blessings sometimes come in strange forms. We don't always realize what it means until we see the result. For me, that blessing came in the form of an elderly gentleman sporting a foot-long cigar, strutting around as if he owned the place. I didn't know the guy from Adam, other than that he was a salesman for Columbia 300®.

At the end of my first PBA tournament in 1985, he walked up to me, grabbed me by the scruff of the neck, and said, "You're going with me."

He informed me that he had seen enough good players struggle. He convinced me to join him and two other PBA bowlers, Dave Husted and Kent Wagner, at another bowling center to work on our games. He was intent on teaching me the art of the free armswing. At first, I was a bit hesitant; but having nothing to lose, I made the smartest decision of my career. I set my ego aside and listened to what he had to say. The first hour was a little perplexing. I had thoughts of opening the parachute and jumping out, but I decided to continue the experiment a little longer. This was the turning point that launched my career into the PBA Hall of Fame.

What a difference an hour makes. Through the kindness of his heart, John Jowdy handed me the keys to a successful career . . . at no charge. Five weeks later, I won my first tournament, which paved my way through a path so many bowlers long to travel, the Firestone Tournament of Champions, followed by 10 subsequent titles.

Jowdy is the blessing of my life. Few before had given so much and asked for nothing in return. Many other players over the years have been the recipients of his talents; they bring to his stable countless titles on the PBA tour. I know he has also had a profound effect on some of the brightest stars on the PWBA tour, including Hall of Fame members Aleta Sill, Betty Morris, and Nikki Gianulias.

Because of John's innate talent, life experience, dedication, and good nature, many have been able to live the dream that they envisioned. Now that his expertise and advice have been compiled in this book, you too have the chance to benefit from his abilities.

So, talent doesn't have to come in the form of physical ability; it can also be a sixth sense that guides a trusting soul to the annals of greatness. John's leadership has guided many of us to the Hall of Fame. Dispensing his time and talent unselfishly earned John the right to walk through those doors as well. He has been inducted into four halls of fame, beginning with his election into the PBA Hall of Fame in 1988. He is the only person ever inducted into the Hall of Fame for coaching. John Jowdy has earned the right to be called the greatest in the world.

With greatest thanks,
David Ozio
PBA Hall of Fame member and
1991 Player of the Year

Preface

Countless books have been published regarding proper bowling techniques. While many are informative and technically beneficial for an aspiring bowler, none offer a more in-depth look at the finer points of the sport than *Bowling Execution*. This book will help you make sense of everything you have learned before this. The principles behind a well-executed shot will finally be easy to implement. You will not only gain a greater understanding of the intricacies of the game, but you will also learn how to apply this information and consistently generate quality shots under any conditions.

Changes in lane maintenance procedures and the ever-increasing potency of urethane balls containing reactive and proactive materials have cast a shadow of doubt on bowling manuals written before the 1990s. With due respect to all the fine coaches and instructors who continue to teach the game as defined before the '90s, many of these methods have been rendered obsolete and present an exercise in futility. Although these teachings may not adversely affect play on soft or doctored conditions, they can seriously inhibit desirable results on conditions that demand quality shots.

My suggestions are based on modern principles and techniques that have been tested and proven on the Professional Bowlers Association (PBA) tour. This book is directed to serious bowlers who prefer to compete on conditions that demand quality shots; it is not for bowlers who remain content in posting unrealistic averages on blocked lanes.

The concepts reflected in this book can be incorporated into any bowler's individual style. They do not necessarily require drastic changes in your game. The focus is on procedures that are essential for obtaining maximum results.

You will simply find the most commonly advocated and effective form of bowling execution I have witnessed, based on more than 50 years of study and observation of the greatest players in the history of the game. As you read, you will recognize problems you are experiencing in your own game. Then, you will find the solutions when you see how I helped pros overcome those same problems.

The pros have to make quality shots. Their execution has to be perfect. This is because PBA lane conditions bear no resemblance to normal house conditions. Oil patterns are vastly different on the PBA tour; break points change from day to day and week to week. There is a premium on quality shots. Speed control and hand positions play major roles. The ability to alter angles is preeminent, not only from day to day and hour to hour, but more often than not, from lane to lane.

Many who jump from standard house conditions to more competitive lane conditions become disenchanted during their "baptism of fire," particularly after posting great records as amateurs in league and tournament competition. Rookies have managed to succeed in other professional sports careers, but instant success in professional bowling is a rare occurrence.

This book is timely for the bowler who is ready to step up to the line to improve bowling skills, not depend on high-tech balls or doctored lane conditions. Across the nation, bowling centers are bringing the challenge back to bowling by promoting "sport" leagues. These leagues reintroduce bowling as a sport, raising the standards by which competitive bowlers are measured. Sport bowlers will again have to rely on their execution and ability to read lanes and make proper adjustments. This book serves as a guide for executing quality shots in the most effective manner, with minimum effort! You can now experience the pride and satisfaction of bowling in honest competitions.

Acknowledgments

If my bowling knowledge, experience, and talents have earned me the privilege of writing this book, I want to thank those that were instrumental in my development and success as a coach and writer.

First and foremost, I would like to thank the Columbia 300 bowling ball family, a company I have been associated with for over 40 years. Columbia afforded me the opportunity to attend tournaments, professional as well as amateur, throughout the United States and other areas of the world. I want to particularly thank the late founders of the company, Mr. and Mrs. Roger Zeller and Mr. Zeller's successor Ronald Herrmann, for their support and friendship. I was, and continue to be, treated more as a family member than as an employee. The management that guided my path in the earlier years at Columbia included Pepper Martin and John Rizzo. Currently, I am truly fortunate to be serving under the dynamic and perceptive leadership of President Mike Allbritton and Vice-President Roger Vessell.

Three of the most noted bowling writers in America, Dick Evans, Joe Lyou, and Chuck Pezzano, deserve recognition for their encouraging words and insightful tips, as well their friendship.

My deep appreciation to PBA President Steve Miller and the PBA staff, particularly Kirk Von Krueger, Beth Marshall, and Russ Twoey, for their wholehearted support in arranging photo shoots of the world's greatest bowlers and full cooperation in other matters so pertinent to the development of this book.

Acknowledgments

Tom Kouros, author of *Par Bowling* and, in my opinion, the most knowledgeable individual in bowling, has my sincere thanks for volunteering vital material, thereby making this book more informative.

Other generous contributors to my book who get my thanks are Roger Dalkin and the American Bowling Congress (ABC); *Bowling Digest*; Bill Vint of *Bowling Magazine*; John Fantini, *Bowling This Month* magazine; and Jim Dressel, *Bowlers Journal International*.

My special thanks to Jerry Francomano for sharing his expertise on measuring and fitting bowling balls.

Special thanks to Columbia 300's Danny Speranza for his keen insight regarding the structure of bowling balls—how they react and the affect they have on the lanes.

Thanks also to Mo Pinel and MoRich Enterprises for their contribution and support.

Thanks to my good friend Rolf Gauger, one of America's top-flight instructors, for his input and support in making this book possible.

I want to express my sincere gratitude to all the Professional Men's Bowling Association bowlers who contributed their time to make this book more interesting, including Dave Arnold, Mike Aulby, Tommy Baker, Chris Barnes, Parker Bohn III, Roger Bowker, Jason Couch, Tim Criss, Norm Duke, Brian Himmler, Marshall Holman, Steve Hoskins, Dave Husted, Mika Koivuniemi, Amleto Monacelli, David Ozio, Rick Steelsmith, Brian Voss, and Pete Weber.

I want to thank Commissioner John Falzone of the Professional Women Bowlers Association with very special thanks to the players that contributed their time and efforts: Kim Adler, Carolyn Dorin-Ballard, Leanne Barrette, Anne Marie Duggan, Michelle Feldman, Cara Honeychurch, Kelly Kulick, Wendy Macpherson, and Robin Romeo Mossontte.

Last, but not least, I'd like to thank everyone at Human Kinetics, particularly Laura Hambly and Ed McNeely, for their patience, guidance, and assistance in making this assignment an easier and most enjoyable endeavor.

1

Establishing a Preshot Comfort Zone

The "comfort zone" is the foundation for competition at your highest level. It is the combination of a relaxed mind, correct ball position, and correct starting position. Through knowledge and practice, you can achieve these essential objectives, which help put you in that special moment—the signal to begin your approach.

The comfort zone can best be described as beginning your approach with tunnel vision—a state of mind exuding confidence in the task at hand. It involves the relaxation of both mind and body, which makes it possible to repeat shot after shot in your best form. Relaxation must reign from the moment you pick up your ball to the moment you step up to the approach and assume your stance.

Stance

Stance is the preparation for a proper approach. It is a comfort zone that you can achieve by learning and implementing both proper ball position and proper starting position, which are the ingredients for the beginning of a quality execution. The comfort zone is a moment of relaxation with respect to the weight and position of the ball and proper alignment of the feet and shoulders. Consider the moment you assume a well-positioned stance to be your signal to execute a quality shot.

An ideal stance is an erect position with the knees slightly flexed. All the weight should be evenly distributed on the feet, which are no more than three inches apart (figure 1.1a). An erect posture is a positive asset to a free armswing, one that provides a great pendulum drive (figure 1.1b). A free armswing is absolutely free of muscle control. This type of swing is propelled by the weight of the ball and generated from the shoulder. A free armswing is the soundest method of execution and helps in maintaining rhythm and consistency. (The free armswing is addressed in further detail in chapter 3.)

Figure 1.1 Dave Arnold illustrates a well-balanced stance, with *(a)* the weight evenly distributed and *(b)* knees slightly flexed.

Ball Position

One type of ball position is recommended, but there are variations that bowlers can use. Bowlers often deviate from standard styles because they have not received proper instruction. If, by chance, a bowler becomes successful with an unorthodox style, it is the exception, not the rule. On the other hand, most serious bowlers prefer to build their games on a solid foundation and grow and adapt from there. It is far wiser to emulate the majority of bowlers, past and present, who achieved superstar status by performing in textbook fashion.

Textbook Ball Position

Textbook ball position finds the elbows resting close to the hips (figure 1.2). The ball is nested in the right palm supported by the left hand

Figure 1.2 Right-hander Chris Barnes demonstrates proper ball position, with the elbows close to the hips and the ball held slightly right of the center of the body.

about waist high and slightly right of the center of the body for right-handed bowlers (opposite for left-handed bowlers). Use a soft upward pushaway and completely relax all muscles to allow the ball to descend by gravity on its own weight into the backswing. Maintain a comfortable ball position before the pushaway. The placement of the ball must permit an easy, undeterred pushaway.

Right-handed bowlers with average- to large-sized hips can hold the ball slightly to the right of the hips. This eliminates the need for a circled backswing. (The circled backswing curls around the buttocks and necessitates realignment to keep the swing line closer to the body.) American Bowling Congress Hall of Famer Therm Gibson developed and popularized this placement.

Holding the ball to the right is not only for those with average to large hips. Many slender-build bowlers, such as PBA star Dave Husted, also hold the ball to the right and demonstrate flawless armswings. You should use whatever position allows your ball to go into the downswing and fall into place directly in line with the body.

Naturally, the foregoing applies the same to women as to men. The average woman's hips are proportionately wider than the average man's hips; consequently, a woman more likely needs to hold her ball slightly to the right to accomplish the free armswing. There are, of course, exceptions to this. Marion Ladewig, generally regarded as the greatest female bowler of all time, had a slender figure. However, she still held the ball slightly to the right and possessed one of the most direct armswings in bowling history. Carolyn Dorin-Ballard, Lisa Wagner, Kim Adler, and Wendy Macpherson, four of the top players on the ladies professional circuit, also accomplish exemplary straight armswings by holding the ball slightly to the right. See figure 1.3.

Variations on Textbook Ball Position

When it comes to stance, there are as many variations as there are bowlers. Although it is important to start out by following the classic position as described earlier, it is also important to make adjustments as needed. The goal is to find a position that's best for you and your game.

Remember, comfort rules! You *must* remain relaxed. Consistency is the desired intention, so it is wise to assume a stance that does not vary from shot to shot. You can achieve this by placing the ball in the same position at the start of each approach. You can keep it in the middle of your body or off to one side if you have wide hips. For players who are plagued with extremely high backswings, I suggest holding the ball low with arms extended, followed by a soft upward shove to create a free

Figure 1.3   Wendy Macpherson positions the ball slightly to the right of her hips to produce a free armswing.

fall of the ball. The position of the hand depends on the amount of hook or the type of roll you are trying to achieve. One of the most helpful tips for maintaining consistency is to keep the elbows nested into your hips, regardless of how high or low you start the pushaway.

Classic players (classic because they perform in textbook fashion) like Parker Bohn III, Chris Barnes, David Ozio, and Brian Voss hold the ball close to their body, slightly above their waist with elbows at their sides, and with the elbows firmly entrenched against the hips. It must be noted that these superstars benefit greatly from placing their arms against their hips to maintain consistency in their pushaways.

Mike Aulby employs a unique method in his starting position. His starting point is high above his head. He slowly lowers the ball to a waist-high position, then pushes up and away into a smooth, free armswing. Mike uses this unorthodox method simply because he has found that this type of pushaway is most comfortable for him. But, it is not advisable to emulate his method of execution.

Pete Weber's method is in direct contrast to that of Aulby's. Pete begins his stance with the ball about chest high. He pushes the ball away in a downward path and pulls the ball back with an extreme tilt, thus creating an unusually high backswing. Weber acquired this method of execution by virtue of necessity. He began at a very early age and, because he was short, used this style to generate speed. Although Weber has perfected this technique through years of repetition, it is not recommended.

An erect position is recommended and is recognized as a standard, but it is not standard for everyone. Several top performers in professional ranks operate from a low crouch. Although this method normally prohibits a free armswing and creates the possibility of rearing up on the release, it is a trademark of several PBA stars. The most notable, Marshall Holman, begins his stance with knees slightly flexed. He bends over from the waist, lowers his arms and hands approximately knee high (figure 1.4), and then draws the ball into the backswing. Although he controls the ball through a short backswing, he has the uncanny ability to exercise a muscle-free forward swing that is propelled from the shoulder. Again, this is not a recommended practice. This is an individual style developed by one of the greatest bowlers in the game.

Bob Learn sets up in a similar style to Holman's, with one exception. Learn bowls from a low crouch and muscles his armswing. Although he has enjoyed a fine career, this method of execution places severe strain on the hand, forearm, and shoulder and is not recommended for any aspiring bowler.

During his heyday in the '50s, '60s, and '70s, Hall of Famer Carmen Salvino held the ball with his elbows at his belt line and his ball about shoulder high. His thumb was at a 1 o'clock position, well under the ball. Salvino then pushed the ball out and away and uncorked one of the most powerful balls of his era. Later in his career, Salvino altered his stance. He held his ball with his right hand fully suspended at his side and initiated his pushaway and approach by shoving the ball up with his left hand into a ball-weighted swing. In the early '90s, Wayne Webb adopted the Salvino style and enjoyed a mild degree of success.

Figure 1.4 Although an erect posture is recommended, Marshall Holman has had great success starting from a low crouch.

Roger Bowker, a five-time PBA titlist, has one of the most unusual stances in the game. A confirmed muscle bowler, Bowker addresses the pins from an erect position with his bowling arm extended completely at his side. He begins his approach with a pulled backswing, completely muscled through the forearm, and delivers in a similar manner throughout the forward swing. Bowker's five championships defy the logic of the free armswing theory, proving again that the sports world is sprinkled with winners who succeed despite performing against the book.

Starting Position

There are three sets of dots on the approach. The first set is 2 inches from the foul line. The next two sets are 12 feet back from the foul line and another 15 feet from the foul line. (See figure 1.6 on page 11.) These dots on the approach serve as a guide for a starting point. The 12-foot dots are generally recommended for four-step bowlers and the 15-foot mark for five-step players.

Determining Starting Distance From Foul Line

There are three steps in determining your starting position:

1. With your back to the pins, walk from the foul line to the starting position, stretching and extending the last step to simulate your slide in a normal approach.

2. Repeat the same procedure, but this time face the pins and do your approach so that you end up near the foul line.

3. Place your starting point a few inches behind the first set of dots on the approach and do a four-step approach. Repeat this process and make the proper adjustments to place the sliding toe within a couple of inches from the foul line.

Taller bowlers are naturally inclined to take longer steps. For instance, during the mid-'80s, Del Warren, a 6-foot, 5-inch bowler, was struggling with his game. Warren began his approach with his heels dangling off the approach. He took five long steps to the foul line in robotic manner, with no visible rhythm or timing. He sought my help and I immediately altered his stance by moving him all the way up to the first set of dots on the approach. I changed his approach from five steps to four and shortened his steps by half. Within an hour, Warren developed one of the smoothest approaches on tour.

Generally, a shorter, quicker pace is far more advantageous for a rhythmic approach than longer, calculated steps. This subject will be addressed further in chapter 4.

Aligning Feet and Shoulders to Target

The cardinal rule for proper bowling execution is this: The bowling arm *must* follow the line of the body, regardless of the angle of the shot. Proper alignment *always* begins with the shoulders and feet. The shoul-

Perfecting the Stance

Mistakes	Modifications
1. Body is too rigid.	**1.** Relax the body by taking deep breaths.
2. Knees are locked.	**2.** Bend knees slightly to release tension in the lower body.
3. Back is arched.	**3.** Do not arch back. This is unnatural and places the body in an awkward position.
4. Toes, shoulders, and body are not aligned to the target area.	**4.** Align toes, hips, and shoulders.

ders and feet must be directly in line with the desired target. In other words, face your target. The feet determine the path of the approach. Any misdirection of the feet can be disastrous. Picture a fire truck driven by two steering mechanisms: one driving the front wheels, the other maneuvering the rear wheels. If the front driver makes a right turn and the rear driver does not correspond, the result is total chaos.

Either the left big toe, the right big toe, or the instep can mark the position of the feet to determine how far left or right you want to position your feet at the start of the approach. Some bowlers place the center of the toe on a certain board; others measure the boards with the inner part of the foot. There is no specific standard of measurement, as long as it is a set pattern, it should work for you. The primary rule is to align the toes and shoulders to the target.

For right-handers, any attempt to swing the ball out to an area outside the second arrow (opposite for left-handers) with the shoulder line perpendicular and feet parallel to the foul line results in pulling the shot. Lining up for strike shots is similar to a stance for 7-pin or 10-pin conversions. You move to a cross-lane position and walk in that direction. Any attempt to address these corner pins with the shoulder line and feet parallel to the foul line will result in a blown spare.

Point the feet and shoulders in direct line to the intended target with utter disregard for your alignment to the foul line. For example, when you are playing the second arrow, down and in, the right shoulder must align with the 10th board (figure 1.5a). When you're playing a deep inside angle (in which the ball is laid down on the 25th board at the foul line to reach a break point at the 10th board), the feet, torso, and shoulder must be aligned in that direction (figure 1.5b). (The *break point* is the area on the lane where the ball begins its entry to the pocket. It is 15 feet from the pocket for a right-handed bowler and the same distance from the 1-2 pocket for left-handed bowlers. In bowling jargon, this is considered *opening up the lane.*) All shots should be performed with the arm and torso square to the desired mark. Anything less will result in misdirection or a pull in the armswing.

Not only is it advantageous to spot a target from the foul line to the arrows, but as many top players do, it also helps to draw an imaginary line from the arrows to the break point, as shown in figure 1.6. As high-powered bowling balls have made the break point easier to predict, this

Figure 1.5 David Ozio aligns his right shoulder *(a)* with the 10th board for a down-and-in shot and *(b)* with the 25th board to play a deep, inside angle.

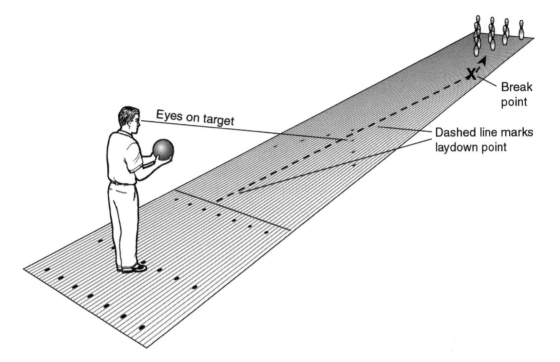

Figure 1.6 A good method of alignment is to spot a target from the foul line to the arrows, then draw an imaginary line from the target board to the break point.

method of alignment has become standard. Although the arrows are the targets for determining the ball path toward the pins, the break point plays a major role in determining strike percentage.

Comfortable and Rhythmic Approach

When aiming to establish a preshot comfort zone, remember that relaxation is the key. During foul shot attempts, professional basketball players display one of the most practical forms of relaxation. Notice how a player bounces the ball several times, takes a deep breath, exhales, and immediately flips the ball toward the hoop. In this manner, all muscles are free of tension. I use the words *tension-free* and *comfortable* throughout my coaching as well as throughout this book. After coaching sessions with me, many students profess how effortless it is to bowl game after game and never tire. Those who experienced chronic aches and pains while bowling were relieved of such discomforts after using the techniques I espouse. Enjoy the sport. Keep your body in proper alignment. Let physics and gravity, not muscle, do all the work for you.

Step Up, Line Up, and Go!

Apply the analogy of basketball players as they execute shots. Although they may bounce the ball several times, they set themselves, take a deep breath, exhale, and immediately flip the ball to the net. In bowling, it should be the same. On many occasions, consuming too much time is detrimental and usually creates undesired tension. How many of you have great games yet still don't make the marks you deserve and desire? Great bowlers like Earl Anthony, Mark Roth, Marshall Holman, Pete Weber, and Walter Ray Williams use minimum time in their stances. They select their starting positions, line up their feet, and start their approaches. Pick your starting point, face your target, take a deep breath, exhale, and start your approach without delay. One of my best students, a PBA member, has yet to make his mark in PBA regional competition despite the fact that he possesses an outstanding physical game. To date, he has failed to overcome the tension that mounts as he overprepares on the approach. My advice, to borrow a slogan, is "Just do it!"

Approach Habits of the Pros

The positioning of the ball and proper alignment of the feet and shoulders constitute the physical aspects of a proper stance, but we need to remember that there is a mental aspect as well. A bowler must commence the stance with a clear mind.

Although fundamentals developed through muscle memory become ingrained, this is no assurance that all systems are go. Despite seemingly complete preparation, numerous bowlers have developed idiosyncrasies that set them apart from others. For example, some of the PBA's most seasoned veterans have quirky lapses in their stances. The most prominent that comes to mind is Barry Asher, one of the greatest talents to ever grace the professional ranks. Although Asher racked up 10 national titles in an abbreviated career, he reached a period in his career when he had extreme difficulty in starting his approach. He would rock back and forth, stutter, back off—as many as three to six times. He could not motivate his feet into the approach. No matter how hard he tried, nothing seemed to help.

On a flight home after a PBA tournament in which he lost by one 10-pin, Asher picked up a sport magazine that featured a psychologist who was also a hypnotist. The sport psychologist's clients included top names in all sports. Upon arriving home, he made an appointment with this psychologist for the next day. Asher made more than 35 visits, yet he was unable to overcome his problem. He did manage to win eight more titles. Unfortunately, the problem became so distressing, he chose to retire from the PBA tour in the prime of his career. It is one of the most tragic stories in PBA history.

Asher bowled league and senior tournaments years later, but never returned to the regular tour. In 1985, he captured the ABC All-Events crown, but because of his inability to keep pace, his team finished bowling 90 minutes later than the other teams. At any rate, Barry's All-Events title qualified him for the U.S. team for the FIQ world competition in England. (FIQ stands for Federation Internationale des Quilleurs—International Bowling Federation.) Barry, easily the best bowler on the American team, continued to be plagued by his inability to start his approach and was asked to withdraw from competition. Today, Asher occasionally competes on the senior tour. He bowls in leagues on a regular basis, averaging 230 and over. Nonetheless, to this day, he continues to experience difficulty in starting his approach.

Bad habits, particularly those created by mental blocks, are seemingly impossible to break. Yet, some people move on despite them.

PBA Hall of Fame member George Pappas was also notorious for peculiar characteristics in his stance. Pappas, unquestionably one of the best clutch bowlers in the game, was cool under fire and a virtual cinch to strike in crucial situations. Nevertheless, while addressing pins in his stance, he took excessive time in starting his approach. He developed a habit of twisting and rolling his shoulders, repeating this seemingly nervous twitch two or three times and consuming 20 to 25 seconds before placing the ball into the pushaway. Like Asher, Pappas won 10 titles, including the Firestone Tournament of Champions. After his retirement from the regular PBA tour, Pappas became a successful proprietor and occasionally takes time off to compete on the senior tour with great success.

Ernie Schlegel is the slowest bowler on the PBA tour. Perhaps this can be attributed to his excessive readiness. Schlegel goes through a series of mental preparations while he addresses pins. He took such excessive time on TV, the PBA was forced to pass a rule requiring bowlers to begin their approach within 25 seconds or face a $25 fine for each violation.

Mark Roth, recently accorded the honor as one of the Top 20 Bowlers of the 20th Century by *ABC Bowling Magazine,* took little or no time to go into action. His incredible record disproves the old adage of "haste makes waste." Roth picked up his ball, looked down at his starting position, and without hesitation, raced to the foul line to the tune of 34 PBA national titles!

Proper bowling execution is based on the coordination of arms and feet in flowing motion. This is the key for precise timing. Focus on the job at hand, exhale, and without hesitation, take the first step. Activate your movements in rhythm and execute the entire process until the release point. Through knowledge and practice, you can achieve that special moment, your signal to begin your approach.

Visualizing Success

Physical talent is the primary ingredient of any athlete. However, in bowling, physical talent alone is not enough. There are thousands of bowlers who possess outstanding physical talent, yet they never reach the heights they desire. Amateur bowlers with incredible physical games, many averaging over 220, flounder and seem lost when faced with challenges in unfamiliar territory. Ever-changing lane conditions such as dry heads, oil carry-down, changing break points, excessive oil in favored zones, and other variables in lane maintenance can confuse and humble even the best, regardless of their talent. This bewilderment is compounded when they leave familiar house conditions for tournaments.

Not too surprising, many top-rated pros are also flustered by these circumstances. The reason for this perplexity is bowlers' failure to recognize the importance of developing the mental dimension in their games. Therein lies the disparity separating amateurs and less successful pros from those who earn a living in professional bowling ranks. In chapter 1, while learning the very beginning of what makes up the physical aspect of our game, we saw the importance of relaxation in creating a preshot comfort zone. The main ingredients for this are the physical aspects; equally important, however, is the mental aspect of relaxation. The point is that no matter what point of the physical game we are talking about, the mental aspect is right there begging for our attention. Therefore, it seems appropriate to take time now to more clearly identify some aspects of the mental game. Then, as you move into chapter 3 and learn about the pushaway and the armswing, it will seem more natural to remember the relaxation component. As you move through this book, recognizing both the physical and the mental aspects of the game will become second nature.

Many top amateurs in the country have tested the waters on the PBA tour. Many succeeded, but the majority have returned to the greener pastures and easier pickings of higher scores and cash found in megabucks tournaments and other amateur events. However, there is a price to pay. Although the huge prize funds are tempting, megabucks promoters do not permit former PBA members to compete if they have won a national title. Consequently, bowlers are faced with a difficult choice: an opportunity to bowl for a huge sum of money against weaker competition or the distinction of a PBA title against the world's best players. Winning a title is the goal of every PBA player. Given an option of the money or a title, a professional bowler would prefer the title every time. Every bowler wants to know the magic formula for winning. Again, the answer is a combination of physical talent *and* mental ability.

Bowling is a totally offensive game; it has no defense position. As with golf, it depends entirely on individual performance. The deciding factor in performances between bowlers of equal ability is the mental state of the participants.

What constitutes a sound mental game, one that distinguishes winners from also-rans? It can be broken down into the following qualities: awareness and intelligence, concentration, self-confidence, ability to read lanes, and knowledge of equipment.

Awareness and Intelligence

Awareness and intelligence are two important keys to success. Awesome physical strength can sometimes be beneficial, but the better bowler will play to the demands of the lanes and deliver accordingly. It becomes your choice, a matter of brains versus brawn. One principle remains steadfast: The lane conditions prescribe the proper attack for scoring, no matter who or how great the bowler may be. This must be the paramount thought process. You take what the lanes permit. You cannot overcome lane conditions on a consistent basis unless you adjust to the lane conditions. Perhaps you may get away with one or two deliveries that are not conducive to the conditions at hand, but, as a general rule, you will ultimately fail.

Unfortunately, many aspiring bowlers believe that excessive revolutions are the answer to successful execution. They revel at the sight of the ball crossing 10 to 18 boards in a wide-arcing trajectory, then booming back off the second or third board at the break point and splattering pins in all directions. I refer to this as a Hollywood shot. The strikes are exciting, but this is the toughest path to success. This type of delivery is reminiscent of golfers who smash uncontrollable drives in excess of 300 yards yet wind up strokes behind those who control 235- to 250-yard tee shots. There is some truth to the old adage "the shortest distance between two points is a straight line." This is not to suggest that a straight ball in bowling is superior to a hook; it merely indicates that an effective hook is one with sufficient drive to carry the 5-pin. The defining word here is *control*. Short hooks are easier to control and have a higher carrying percentage. Also, they are less likely to produce difficult spare shots.

"Professional women bowlers may not have big, hooking balls with a super amount of revolutions. For some, these are the only things that garner respect or admiration as a bowler. I am a self-proclaimed 'tweener'— more accurate but less powerful than a cranker, and less accurate but more powerful than a straight shooter. The tweeners are a silent minority, even more so among women bowlers. We are constantly molding our games to the condition of the moment, only rarely matching our 'A' games to an oil pattern. Because we cannot take advantage of unique lane conditions, we must be more accurate, more open to changes, and more levelheaded for making quick decisions than other bowlers. When people think of bowling superstars, my name may not come up, but I hope when it is all said and done that people will respect my game for what I have been able to accomplish through all of my hard work, both physically and mentally."

Kim Adler
Top PWBA pro with 14 titles

Concentration

Concentration is the ability to focus on the subject at hand. In bowling, the prime objective is to put the ball in the pocket. This must be uppermost in the thought process.

Kim Adler's focus and accuracy have helped her become a successful pro.

Many observers, including Hall of Famer Johnny Petraglia and former PBA tournament director Harry Golden, consider Don Johnson to be the greatest clutch bowler they've ever seen. Johnson admitted that he was far less talented than most of his competitors, yet he managed to win 26 PBA titles before injuries forced him into retirement. His focus was so intense that he was oblivious to any sounds or distractions that would have rattled average bowlers, especially in crucial situations.

Mike Aulby demonstrates the trait of utter concentration. Aulby, one of the most disciplined bowlers in history, can be matched or surpassed in ability by numerous players. Nevertheless, he is the only player to date that has captured all five major titles: the PBA National, the Touring Players Championship, the U.S. Open, the Tournament of Champions, and the ABC Masters. He is the *only* player to have won the coveted ABC Masters *three* times. One of his shining moments occurred in 1995 when he completed the Triple Crown cycle by winning the Tournament of Champions the way he so often does: by striking out in the 10th frame when all three strikes were needed. This is further evidence of Aulby's extraordinary mental toughness.

Amleto Monacelli has recorded 18 titles in his career. With all due respect to his tremendous talent, Amleto's cerebral approach to the game has been one of his greatest assets. Amleto was the top seed on the ABC televised show at the 1988 Showboat Invitational. His concentration on the tough scoring condition was truly visible. This occurred during an era in which PBA telecasts were producing unusually low scores. PBA lane maintenance men were flabbergasted at their inability to overcome the problem of lighting effects on oil patterns. On this particular day, the scores of the first three matches were embarrassingly low. The oil carry-down made it virtually impossible to hit the pocket with any consistency, and strikes were almost nonexistent. In fact, Monacelli, whose forte is a powerful hook, was bewildered during the first five frames. His hook ball was ineffective, either overreacting or simply skidding. By the same token, his opponent was equally puzzled. At the end of the fifth frame, with both players struggling and the game fairly even, Monacelli displayed his mental proficiency by reverting to a straight shot, direct to the pocket. Although strikes were still nonexistent, Amleto managed high counts and easy spares. He endured and emerged victorious with, believe it or not, a 158 game! It was not pretty but it was good enough to cart off a title.

So what can you do to reach the same level of concentration as successful pros have? One of my favorite suggestions for transforming concentration into reality is to draw a picture in your mind, wherein your strike shot enters the pocket and demolishes the pins. This is the power of positive thinking. Think positive and the results are more apt to be positive. Also, as you are seated and awaiting your turn to bowl, try to recall your successful achievements and how you accomplished them. More important, think of how you felt, and regain that same feeling you had at that time. Simply put, all these suggestions are based on positive thinking, the most basic element for concentration and confidence.

Here are some additional tips from select members of the Ladies Professional Bowling tour who have exhibited great powers of concentration:

1. **Treat each shot the same, focusing on execution, not outcome.**

"I try not to treat one shot any differently from another but rather focus on making the best shot I can each and every time; by doing so, you focus on execution rather than outcome. Chances are that if you execute well, the score will take care of itself."

Cara Honeychurch
2000 PWBA Rookie of the Year

2. **Relax and stay positive.**

"I worked with Dr. Eric Lasser last year clearing my mind of negative thoughts in crucial situations. I try to stay as positive as possible. Sometimes it's hard but I have a few things I repeat over and over to myself to help me relax and keep positive. On TV I always make sure to breathe a lot. This helps me to relax and helps me maintain my focus."

Carolyn Dorin-Ballard
2000 PWBA Player of the Year runner-up

3. **Don't get mad; get even.**

"Bowling made its first appearance in the Commonwealth Games in Malaysia in 1998. The Commonwealth Games are similar to the Olympics but for commonwealth countries only. Malaysia had a strong team and was expected to do well; however, they had targeted me as the biggest threat to their success and decided to resort to alternative tactics to distract me. This campaign was called 'Operation Cara' and included such things as the media writing unfavorable things about me in the newspapers and people blowing horns and making other loud noises during my approach. None of these people were reprimanded or asked to leave the venue. As you can imagine, it took a great deal of concentration and belief in myself to be able to overcome such trying circumstances. However, I was able to do so and this resulted in my winning three gold medals. It will always go down in my mind as one of my greatest achievements."

Cara Honeychurch

4. **Take it game by game.**

"My husband, Del Ballard, has influenced me the most in dealing with my mental game. He taught me how to approach a tournament each week, game by game, not day by day. I used to always think ahead and get lost

in the shuffle. He taught me that you cannot win a tournament during the qualification rounds; you win in head-to-head competition. Putting things in perspective allowed me to focus in the right direction."

Carolyn Dorin-Ballard

Confidence

Confidence is the faith in one's ability to perform in clutch situations. Norm Duke has risen to superstar status not only by virtue of his incredible talent but also through his bowling intellect. His thought process, his compliance to lane dictates, and his confidence in the way he attacks the lanes have set him apart from those who lack his mental approach.

Norm Duke's confidence and intense concentration give him an edge over his competitors.

21

Chris Barnes was one of the best amateur bowlers in the world before joining the PBA tour. He became an instant success. His greatest assets are his intellectual method of operation and his supreme confidence. His knack of reading lanes and his willingness to conform to lane dictates, coupled with his magical hand, account for his status as one of the top stars on the PBA tour.

Talent and lane savvy speak for themselves as keys to success. Success breeds confidence. The world is replete with egotists who exude false confidence. They hustle easy pickings and are usually backed by others. Pressure-free, they freewheel and bask in undeserving glory.

Conversely, true confidence is the ability to quietly apply pressure on opponents, à la Earl Anthony during his brilliant career. Anthony caused other bowlers to look over their shoulders as they anticipated his charge. His appearance in championship matches gave him a psychological advantage. He was a study in concentration and could not be counted out until it was mathematically impossible to do so. He seldom missed the opportunity to jump on an opponent's mistake and was a virtual cinch to strike out if an opponent left an opening late in the game.

Carolyn Dorin-Ballard exudes the same demeanor as Earl Anthony does. Although very personable and a friend to everyone off the lanes, she approaches the game with supreme confidence and concentration. On the lanes, Carolyn Dorin-Ballard is all business!

Confidence is a trait that set apart such other superstars as Dick Weber, Don Johnson, Don Carter, and Mark Roth from other bowlers. Weber's warm personality belied his fierce competitiveness. He spoke kindly, smiled, showed appreciation for an opponent's success, acted as the perfect gentleman, then battered his opponents with a barrage of strikes. He whipped them to a pulp and still made them love him.

Johnson was a real pro. He got more out of his game than any bowler in history. He had the guts of a gorilla and made the most radical moves that anyone could imagine. On numerous occasions, Johnson would abandon a deep inside line in favor of an area outside the fifth board, ever confident and never flinching.

Mark Roth, another immortal, turned in one of the greatest examples of confidence I have ever seen at Norwalk, California, in 1977. Bowling against hometown favorite Bobby Fliegman in the title match on television, Roth stepped up in the 10th frame needing three strikes to win by one pin. Mark was forced to finish his 10th frame on a lane he hadn't come remotely close to striking on in his previous four tries. He uncorked three perfect strikes to take the match. Roth exuded knowledge, concentration, and confidence—ingredients that formulate a proper mental preparation.

So how can you build and maintain the same level of confidence as these successful pros? When you lose confidence in your game, how can you rebuild it? The following are a few suggestions from the pros:

1. Identify problems in your game and strive to fix them.

"The more I learn about something from every angle, the more confidence I have. Usually if you think you have problems with your game physically, it is really something mental, and if you are mentally confused with your game, concentrate on the physical game because there's usually something wrong there. Have fun, set new goals, realize it is a time of renewal and change. Go with the flow; do not fight it, just go with it."

Kim Adler
Top PWBA pro with 14 titles

2. Get back on track with changes you believe in.

"When you lose confidence in your performances, you have to make changes . . . changes that will put you back on track. You not only make changes . . . you have to have faith in the changes in order to regain confidence."

Marshall Holman
PBA Hall of Famer

3. Recall instances in which you successfully overcame a difficult situation.

"If I have lost my confidence there is usually a reason for it, and so the first thing I do is identify what part of my game is suffering and attempt to rectify the issue. Confidence is a state of mind and takes time to build. If I feel that I am lacking confidence I will think of all the situations throughout my bowling career where I have triumphed in challenging circumstances and what I did to overcome those difficulties."

Cara Honeychurch
2000 PWBA Rookie of the Year

4. Review tapes of yourself bowling at your best.

"If I start to lose confidence, I watch a lot of my TV shows. Especially those in which I feel I was bowling my best. I also bowl everything I can during this time to get that one great tournament, or block, or an overall feeling that things are getting better. Confidence is all in how you feel about yourself."

Carolyn Dorin-Ballard
2000 PWBA Player of the Year runner-up

5. Take pride in your accomplishments. Don't dwell on mistakes.

"I have been Player of the Year runner-up for four years. Although I have learned to take great pride in this accomplishment, the last few years had me looking at what I might be lacking to achieve this goal. I have to take pride in what I achieve, not dwell on what I do not accomplish. If you take pride and joy in what you do well, this is a great foundation for self-confidence."

Carolyn Dorin-Ballard

Carolyn Dorin-Ballard approaches the game with supreme confidence and concentration.

Ability to Read Lanes

Awareness and intelligence, concentration, and confidence are components that make up half of a bowler's mental game. The ability to read lanes and conform to what the lane dictates as well as knowledge of equipment are equally important.

Amateur and league bowlers are accustomed to lanes that are conditioned for high scores. Though it may not be the case everywhere, most proprietors cater to customers who derive pleasure from posting high averages. This is not meant as an indictment of proprietors who want to please their clientele but is simply an attempt to stress the simplicity of house conditions compared to those on the PBA tour and those of megabucks events.

Reading lanes is probably the most difficult task facing bowlers. Oil patterns are not detectable by the naked eye. Oil is colorless, and seeking a line to the pocket is like running an obstacle course blindfolded. In golf, sand traps, high grass, trees, water, and other hazards are clearly visible, but bowlers are not afforded these luxuries. Bowlers have to take risks, gamble, and speculate based on unseen obstacles.

The changing oil patterns are due primarily to increased activity in certain playing areas. Urethane balls that are designed to create greater friction on the lanes wreak havoc on lane conditioning. The emergence of bowling balls with advances such as Reactive Resin™ and Proactive™ coverstocks has further complicated oil patterns. Although these new weapons have been a boon to players who throw harder and straighter shots, they have further complicated the process of choosing proper equipment. In previous eras changes in speed, hand position, ball weight, or ball surface were required, but bowlers today must resort to several alterations to be competitive. Carry percentage has become a big factor in a bowler's ability to detect a workable break point. The break point is the paramount ingredient for separating strikes from 9-counts. Therein lies the significance of reading lanes and knowing the proper equipment to use.

In reading the lanes, right-handers must calculate adjustments for hitting the 1-3 pocket; left-handers must calculate adjustments for hitting the 1-2 pocket. These pockets are 60 feet away from the bowler with skid, roll, and hook at different angles against undetectable oil patterns. Golfers can recover from errant shots, and baseball pitchers have the luxury of eight other teammates to bail them out of critical situations. But bowlers can pound the 1-3 pocket continually with no redeeming reward for their efforts. Stubborn 4-pins, 10-pins, 7-pins, and now, because of reactive balls, 9-pins have cropped up to further discourage bowlers.

As a rule, bowlers test all lanes by delivering the first ball down the 10th board in a straight line. The condition of the oil pattern will dictate the amount of hook one can expect. Follow this test by exploring other areas on the lanes. The more the ball hooks, the farther left you should move your feet. Move left or right according to the amount of hook you are experiencing. Begin by moving from the second arrow to the second or third board, then back to the third or fourth arrow, playing each angle from a different starting point on the approach. See figure 2.1.

If a ball is laid down on the 10th board, crosses the arrows at the 10th board, and ends up at the 10th board on the pin deck, it has a zero hook power. If it ends up on the 17th board, it is in the pocket and has recorded a hook power of seven boards.

If a ball is laid down on the 12th board and crosses the 10th board (second arrow), it will end up at the fourth board if it doesn't hook. Most professional players divide the length of the lane (60 feet) into four separate divisions of 15 feet. A nonhooking ball that is laid down on the 12th board and crosses the 10th board at the arrows will hit the 8th board halfway down the lane, hit the 6th board at 45 feet, and cross the 4th board at the pin deck. However, an average-hooking ball will reach a break point at approximately 45 feet, break left toward the pins, then enter the pocket at the 17th board.

Hitting the pocket is no assurance for strikes. The entry angle takes precedence over anything related to proper execution. Unfortunately, young bowlers place great emphasis on power balls with excessive revolutions. Although these deliveries create excitement with their destructive force, they are reminiscent of the old adage, "Those who live by the sword die by the sword." True, bowling balls unleashed with brute power create bigger pockets. On the other hand, they tend to leave ungodly splits, such as the 2-8-10 and other wide-open splits resulting from odd entry angles.

Changing lane conditions necessitate strategic moves laterally on the approach. The moves contract or expand the arc of the ball to provide a more advantageous angle to the pocket. A one-one move means that the feet move one board laterally and one board at the crossing point, either right or left. Two-one, two-two, and other lateral moves are all devised to alter the ball's path to the pocket.

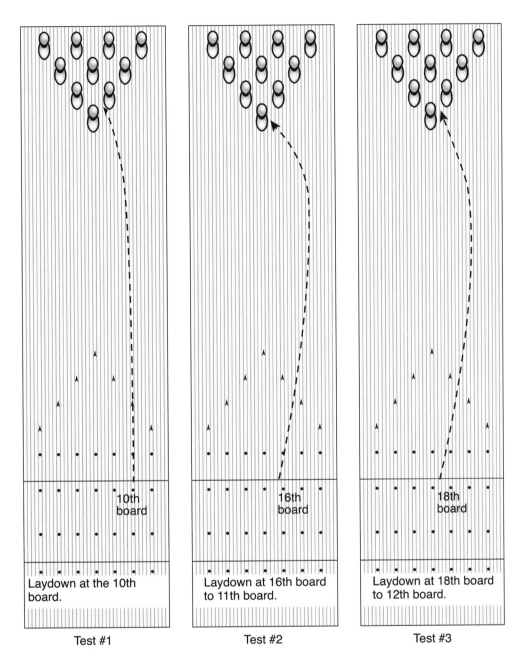

| Test #1 | Test #2 | Test #3 |

Laydown at the 10th board.

Laydown at 16th board to 11th board.

Laydown at 18th board to 12th board.

10th board

16th board

18th board

(continued)

Figure 2.1 Test the lane by delivering the first ball down the 10th board in a straight line. The more the ball hooks, the farther left you should move your feet. Move left or right according to the amount of hook you are experiencing. Begin by moving from the second arrow to the second or third board, then back to the third or fourth arrow, playing each angle from a different starting point on the approach.

27

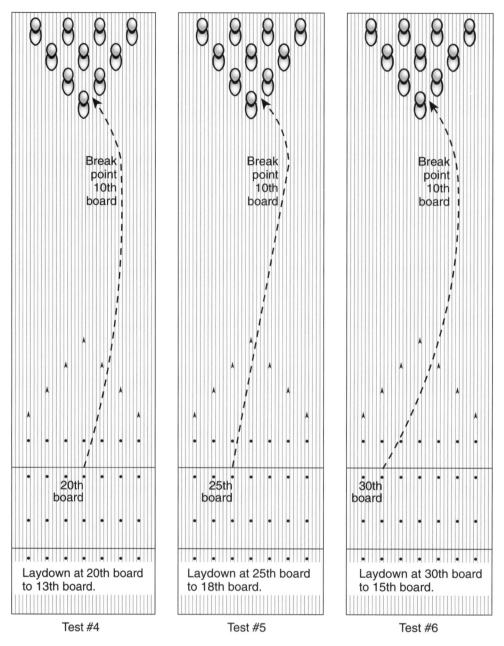

Test #4

Test #5

Test #6

Figure 2.1 *(continued).*

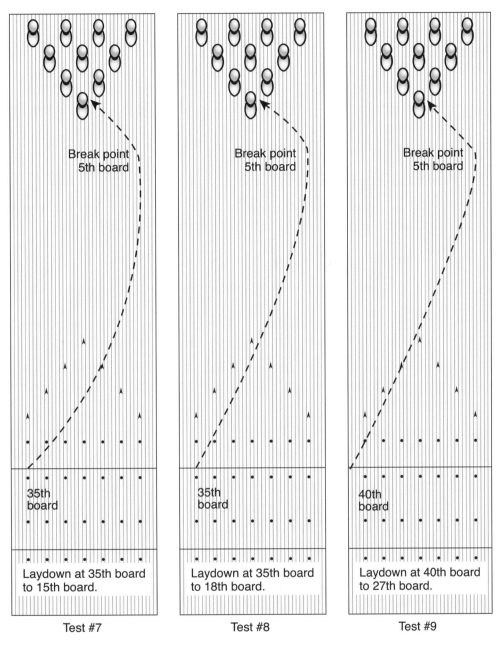

Break point
5th board

35th
board

Laydown at 35th board
to 15th board.

Test #7

Break point
5th board

35th
board

Laydown at 35th board
to 18th board.

Test #8

Break point
5th board

40th
board

Laydown at 40th board
to 27th board.

Test #9

Figure 2.1 *(continued).*

Dry heads (lanes that are dry on the front part of the playing surface) pose problems for players who throw wide hooks because of the high friction of the ball with the lane at the release point. Smart players move left to seek an oil area; others attempt to loft the ball over the heads. I have long objected to lofting the ball far out on the lane. A ball lofted upward is summarily spinning in midair and has a tendency to bounce when contacting the lanes. Consequently, it reacts irregularly on its path to the desired goal. This is addressed in chapter 5.

Checklist for Lining Up

Many bowlers use a checklist for lining up. Here are a few examples (note that these suggestions are opposite for left-handers):

- ☒ Begin with a target line on the 10th board.

- ☒ On dry lanes, move left with your feet and target.

- ☒ On slicker lanes, move right with your feet.

- ☒ On dry heads, move left, find the oil, and play the oil line.

- ☒ When oil areas dry up, make one-one, two-one, and two-two adjustments (that is, one board left with the feet, one board left on the approach, and so on).

- ☒ When oil carries down, the ball will sometimes go through the break point or break a bit late, leaving a weak 10-pin. You have two choices: Move the feet right to catch a break point sooner, or start the approach about two inches farther back on the approach to compensate for the late entry to the pocket.

- ☒ When conditions favor a gutter shot (outside the first arrow), point the shoulder of the throwing arm inward about one or two inches. This creates a feeling of an inside-outside swing and prevents pointing and pulling. It also eliminates gutter balls resulting from open shoulders that fail to close in time.

Remember, hitting the pocket is the primary goal for every bowler. Hitting the pocket with sufficient power to carry is the primary purpose. But always remember that a strong mental approach will ease the task of attaining these objectives.

Knowledge of Equipment

Knowledge of equipment is perhaps 50 percent of the mental aspect for a bowler and is more important than some might believe. On tour, PBA players have access to bowling ball representatives who are thoroughly informed of surfaces, weights, and ball reaction. PBA players rely heavily on these specialists and seek advice from these experts during trying times.

As an amateur bowler, you would be wise to look to the lanes you are going to bowl on to extract all the information possible. Watch the reaction of the ball on every lane condition. Check your equipment's surfaces and weight distribution. There is no guarantee of success when you purchase exotic bowling balls that range from $150 to $275 if you have not become familiar with the equipment. (Advice on choosing proper equipment is covered in chapter 12.) Memorize the reaction of every ball in your arsenal. Is your ball hooking too early in the heads? Is your ball skidding too far? Is it breaking into the pocket too sharply or breaking in behind the 1-3 pocket a bit late? Can you make any of these adjustments by changing hand positions or speed or perhaps by re-aligning your starting positions? To remain competitive, you must learn to read the ball reaction and use the proper equipment. When professional bowlers become unsure of the balls they are using, they are never reluctant to check out the equipment that other successful bowlers use. They are also wise to stand behind competitors and scrutinize the reaction of their balls and the lines they are playing. After all, this is competition.

3

Relaxing the Armswing for Fluid Motion

Bowling instruction books recommend various methods for a proper pushaway and armswing. Some suggest a shorter pushaway; others recommend a fully extended arm with the elbow locked. These diverse theories may present a dilemma for aspiring bowlers. This chapter addresses the different styles of execution and identifies which technique typically provides the best results.

Pushaway

In my experience, a proper pushaway is one that produces a free armswing. A free armswing is a muscle-free swing in which the movement of the arm is generated by the weight of the ball. You accomplish that by holding the ball in the right hand with the left hand supporting it (opposite if you're a lefty). The ball should be close to the body, about waist high (figure 3.1a). Initiate the pushaway with a small arc, forming a curl and going up and out as you enter the downswing (figure 3.1b). Do this arcing motion in a soft, smooth manner. The entire process is contingent on a muscle-free forearm propelling the arcing motion into a weighted swing from the shoulder joint. As the foundation of your

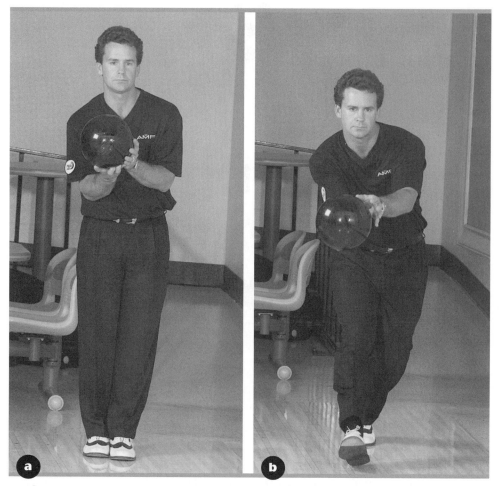

Figure 3.1 Brian Voss (a) holds the ball close to his body, then (b) initiates the pushaway with minimum force from the forearm.

bowling style, this form of execution greatly increases the quality and consistency of your shots.

Pushaway Variations

As previously mentioned, different bowlers sometimes prefer different styles of execution. Some PBA players (Norm Duke, Pete Weber, and Danny Wiseman) resort to shorter pushaways. A shorter pushaway is actually controlled—generally fashioned from a lower position and directed downward rather than in an arc. Other bowlers use the full extension of the arm and higher backswings with great success. This group includes Jason Couch, Steve Hoskins, Amleto Monacelli, and Dave

D'Entremont. Although these men are all power bowlers and deliver extremely explosive strike balls, this does not mean that extended armswings add additional revolutions to a ball. The extended armswing just happens to be their preferred method of execution.

Walter Ray Williams, one of bowling's all-time greats, has garnered more than 30 titles via an end-over-end roll using an extended arm. During the '70s and '80s, Mats Karlsson notched four titles on the PBA tour. The outstanding Swedish star emphasized the fully extended pushaway with a locked elbow. Karlsson's strike ball was average at best, but he was one of the strongest spare shooters of his era. Mika Koivuniemi, an outstanding player from Finland, has proven himself on American soil. He won the 2000 ABC Masters title and has been a consistent contender on the PBA tour. Like Karlsson, Mika uses the fully extended pushaway with a locked elbow. Carmen Salvino was one of the great power bowlers of the '50s, '60s, and '70s. He began his career using an extended pushaway and threw one of the most potent strike balls of his era. During the latter days of his career, he began his stance with his arm fully suspended to his right side. He initiated his pushaway with the aid of his left hand, shoved the ball upward, and permitted the ball to descend on its own weight. Although this is not textbook fashion, it encompasses all the elements of a free swing. These examples demonstrate that professional bowlers have succeeded using different styles of execution. The diverse methods in this phase of the game indicate that there is no set pattern, no absolute correct system.

Correcting Common Errors

Although pushaways can be altered to simplify execution, pushaways that are successful for some can be harmful to others. The early pushaway and the forced pushaway are the most common styles that can wreak havoc on bowlers' games.

Early Pushaway

Error: An early pushaway (that is, placing the ball into position before initiating the first step) will result in an early swing. An early swing commonly prohibits a strong release point. (The release is covered in chapter 5.)

Correction: The pushaway must coincide with the first step in a four-step approach (figure 3.2). The simultaneous movement is the principal factor in developing proper rhythm and timing and in producing a

Figure 3.2 To prevent an early swing, the pushaway must coincide with the first step in a four-step approach.

strong release. It will prevent an early swing and allow you to wait for the descent of the ball in the forward swing. This can only be accomplished if the slide is firmly planted before the release point, an area slightly at or behind the ankle position. This is the strongest leverage point for an ideal release. In an early swing, the ball arrives slightly ahead of the slide, beyond the ankle and shoulder joints. This will considerably weaken the shot. If you are faced with this dilemma you can adjust and improve your game by initiating the first step a fraction of a second before beginning the pushaway. Although this strategy delays the swing, it will assure a greater leverage position.

Perfecting the Pushaway

Mistakes	Modifications
1. Pushaway is muscled, vigorous, and too far out.	**1.** Relax the forearm. Place the burden of weight in the nonbowling hand.
2. It is shorter than the first step.	**2.** Place the ball softly beyond the first step to create greater weight in the swing.
3. It uses a downward projection.	**3.** Push the ball in an upward motion (about four to six inches) to create gravity in the down-swing all the way through the backswing.
4. The ball is pushed right or left of the body.	**4.** Disengage all muscles, push the ball in the direction of the target, and let ball fall into the backswing from its own weight.
5. The ball is tilted on the pushaway.	**5.** Do not tilt until the ball begins to enter the backswing and forces a *natural* tilt.

In a five-step approach, there is one major adjustment. After the first step, *pause* slightly, then proceed. This will prevent any early movement in the pushaway and allow you to synchronize the pushaway with the second step.

Forced Pushaway

Error: A coerced or vigorous pushaway can seriously impair the free armswing and induce a tilt in the pushaway step. This, in turn, can impede the cadence and rhythm in the approach.

Correction: Execute the pushaway in a soft, delicate method, regardless of the manner in which you initiate it. Do not use a vigorous initial thrust in the pushaway; use a silky, easy pushaway with minimum force from the forearm. To influence gravity in the ball's descent, apply the ball in an arcing manner before disengaging all muscles. Although I recommend my over-under theory (addressed later in this chapter), bowlers who subscribe to a suspended armswing (à la Salvino) can produce a quality pushaway by practicing it from a lower position.

Armswing

Armswings can be classified in three manners of execution: free, semicontrolled, and controlled.

Free Armswing

A quality pushaway plays a major role in the execution of one of the most important phases of the game: a free armswing, also known as the pendulum swing (figure 3.3, a-d). Consider the pendulum on a clock. The pendulum swings right, then it swings an equal distance to the left. Picture the top of the pendulum as your shoulder and the body of the pendulum as your arm; you arm moves into the forward swing with force equal to the backward swing, *every time!* This action is an example of physics. The centrifugal force, the weight of the ball, the height of the backswing, and the descent of the forward swing remain constant.

Figure 3.3 Left-hander Parker Bohn III demonstrates the free armswing: *(a)* starting position, *(b)* pushaway, *(c)* backswing, and *(d)* start of the forward swing.

Consider this: Isn't it reasonable to assume that if you eliminate as many of the intangible factors as possible and build your game on a tangible factor, you will have a better game? That's called consistency. Countless times I've heard lamenting bowlers say, "My game lacks consistency." Adopting the free swing as the basis of your game will give you the consistency you've been looking for. You will achieve the same swing every time and develop a firm starting point from which to build and perfect your game.

Why do I consider a free armswing to be the cornerstone for ideal shotmaking? Check the records of any athlete. Other than athletes whose endeavors require brute strength, the most successful contestants are those who perform in a relaxed manner, void of any muscle application. For example, in football, offensive and defensive linemen, linebackers, and fullbacks all rely on brawn and power. Conversely, those who rely on speed and deftness (the cornerbacks, wide receivers, and running backs) use a more mental approach: agility to deceive and mislead their opponents. They achieve this craft through muscle-free

athleticism. Quarterbacks Dan Marino, John Elway, Drew Bledsoe, and Kurt Warner sling precise passes that originate from muscle-free arms and lightning releases.

Basketball players are perhaps the greatest athletes in the world. Seven-footers who specialize in dunking and blocking shots leave basketball fans in awe, but the most exciting players in the NBA are superstars like Vince Carter, Allen Iverson, and Kobe Bryant, who demonstrate muscle-free agility to leave audiences breathless.

The top pitchers in baseball exemplify advantages of muscle-free execution. Randy Johnson, Billy Wagner, and Pedro Martinez deliver fastballs at speeds of 95 miles per hour or faster, whistling rockets via unrestricted arms. Johnson is 6 feet 10 inches tall, lean, and limber. Martinez is 10 inches shorter and loose as a goose. Houston Astros relief artist, Billy Wagner, is small and wiry, yet he disheartens batters with 100-mile-per-hour fastballs.

How do these athletes' techniques relate to bowling? Simply put, a free swing permits a player to release a ball more consistently at the power point than a muscled swing permits. Also, a free swing is far less exhausting and puts less undue strain on the shoulder than a swing that is controlled and generated through the forearm. Superstars like Mike Aulby, Parker Bohn III, Dave Husted, Brian Voss, and David Ozio have exemplified the advantages of free armswings.

Over and Under Drill

One of the most effective keys to initiating a free armswing is the over and under drill. It is a system I developed that has benefited many of my students, past and present. The system not only aids bowlers in developing a free armswing but also facilitates and improves a strong release point.

The drill is simple. It involves two imaginary bars. One imaginary bar is at the starting point and one is at the release point. Place one imaginary bar about four to six inches above the starting ball position. Push the ball over this bar, disengage all muscles in the forearm, and let the ball descend and swing with its own gravitational force. The under aspect of the over and under drill involves releasing the ball under the other bar 12 inches above the foul line. The entire drill is contingent on one's ability to transfer the weight of the ball from the hand to the shoulder, which is the essence of a free armswing. I suggest a few preliminary swings before the pushaway to get a feel of the swing weight from the shoulder joint.

How the Free Armswing Helped David Ozio's Game

Courtesy of ABC Bowling Magazine

David Ozio is a prime example of the benefits of a free armswing. Ozio joined the PBA in 1978 and, although he possessed one of the most graceful games in bowling, he had little to show for it monetarily. In six years (1978 through 1984; he sat out the 1980 season) he won a meager $106,482 in 160 tournaments.

I met Ozio in 1985 at the Greater Los Angeles tournament in Torrance, California. I was arranging a practice at a nearby establishment with David Husted and Kent Wagner, two Columbia staff members. Ozio, a studious bowler, was close by and overheard our conversation. When Wagner, Husted, and I arrived at the workout, Ozio was bowling at the opposite end of the lanes. Eventually, he came over and asked me to explain my free armswing theory. David Ozio possessed one of the smoothest approaches in the game. But despite his impeccable footwork, his release point was weak because of his semicontrolled armswing (addressed later in this chapter). This hampered his ability to execute quality shots on a consistent basis.

The over and under drill was the foundation for my coaching session with Ozio. I began by placing my fingers on his arm at the shoulder joint. I placed my right palm about 20 to 24 inches in a direct line of his right shoulder. I instructed him to hit my palm with the pushaway, relax all the muscles in his forearm, and let the ball descend from its own weight. We repeated this exercise several times until he sensed the flowing sensation of the ball from his shoulder. After 30 minutes with Ozio, I returned to my other students. Within an hour, an excited Ozio came over and expressed disbelief at the improvement in accuracy and pin-carry. The following week, during the practice session at the Showboat Invitational in Las Vegas, we resumed our workouts. Fortunately, Ozio made the finals, finishing high in the standings. He made the finals at the Quaker State Open in Dallas and continued to improve at the next two Florida tournaments. One week later, at the AMF Angle Open in Florissant, Missouri, Ozio won his first title. He won again later that year at the Tucson Open in Arizona. Ozio earned more than $85,000 in the 1985 season, slightly less than half of his entire earnings for his career thus far. He now has 11 titles and more than $1,300,000 in career earnings, was the player of the year in 1991, and was elected to the PBA Hall of Fame in 1995. Ozio is also an advocate of the free armswing.

A true pendulum swing is simply the movement of the arm generated by the weight of the ball. This is the basis for consistency. A sound key for exercising this maneuver is letting the weight of the ball determine the peak of the backswing and the ensuing forward swing until the magic moment—the release point!

Although a muscle-free armswing is the prime objective, the placement of the ball in the pushaway does require a soft muscular application for completion of a quality shot. Place the ball into motion in a slight upward manner. At this point, disengage all muscles, transfer the weight to the shoulder joint, and let gravity govern the height of the backswing and the momentum of the forward swing.

A perfect analogy for a free swing would be to detach the arm at the shoulder, drill a hole in the arm, place ball bearings in the socket, grease it well, reattach the arm to the shoulder with a bolt, then swing all motion from this area.

Free armswings were the trademarks of Tom Hennessey, Dick Ritger, and Joe Joseph. These outstanding players gained ABC Hall of Fame status by virtue of free armswings, ideal timing and rhythm, and other essential traits for maximizing scoring potential without undue exertion. Hennessey, Joseph, and Ritger were not known as power players, yet they held their own against opponents who exhibited thunderous strike balls.

Free armswings in bowling can be likened to the principles demanded in golf. Sam Snead, Gene Littler, and Julius Boros, three of golf's greatest players, exerted minimum effort in their games and relied on muscle-free swings to achieve immortality. On the current PGA Tour, Ernie Els is poetry in motion: He demonstrates effortless, rhythmic, and above all, muscle-free execution. If *you* can master the free armswing, it will signal the beginning of a better game.

Semicontrolled Armswing

I strongly favor the use of a free swing, but I think it is important to present other methods of execution because some bowlers are successful exercising a more controlled swing. A semicontrolled armswing is executed with minimum muscle application. Numerous bowlers have accomplished outstanding results with semicontrolled armswings. Two of the greatest players in the history of the game, Don Carter and Earl Anthony, are renowned for their semicontrolled swings.

A semicontrolled swing is one that is initiated downward or slightly up and controlled by a muscled forearm. Muscle is further applied to pull the ball into the backswing. At this point, all muscles are disengaged and the ball descends on its own weight.

Don Carter, considered by many the greatest bowler ever, demonstrated the epitome of a semicontrolled armswing. He began his approach from a low crouch, bent his elbow, drew the ball back with his forearm into a low backswing, and literally shoved the ball off his shoulder and down the lane. Earl Anthony, the most notable bowler of the modern era, was similar to Carter in several ways. Although Anthony stood more erect, he too applied a short backswing with a slightly bent elbow and, like Carter, pushed the ball down the lane. Not too surprising, Carter and Anthony rarely endured early hooking problems.

Marshall Holman, recently selected as one of the 20 greatest bowlers of the century, addressed the pins with a slight bend in his stance. He extended the ball down with both hands at knee level. Holman initiated his approach by pushing the ball up slightly then pulling it into a low backswing. Ordinarily, this would have resulted in a very early swing, an error that would place the release point *beyond* the leverage area. However, Holman took five short steps in rapid succession. His forward swing was free and smooth and his quick feet *always* set him in position to wait for the ball before the release.

Pete Weber is the most successful contemporary player using a semicontrolled armswing (figure 3.4). To Pete's credit, his forward swing is one of the most fluid in the game, despite the fact that he executes it from an extremely high backswing. The unusual height of the swing can be traced to a pattern he developed in his early teens, a habit compelled by his desire to generate speed. Pete's propensity for initiating his semicontrolled pushaway in a downward path has been a source of irritation in his career and occasionally results in an early swing that hampers his game.

I have had the pleasure of coaching Pete Weber on numerous occasions. I worked with him on his downward pushaway and early tilt, which together produced a release point beyond his ankle. Our objective was to lengthen his swing to consume enough time to place the release point at or behind the ankle, the ideal release point. The focus of our practice sessions included these two recommendations:

1. I suggested a slight upward motion to compensate for his downward pushaway. This was intended to lengthen his swing.

2. To address the early tilt, I suggested he use a more erect approach and keep his shoulders back before he tilted into the backswing. The arcing movement of the ball, together with the elimination of the early tilt, delayed the swing enough to provide the proper release point.

Figure 3.4 Some players, like Pete Weber, prefer a semicontrolled armswing.

Although Weber has been successful with a semicontrolled swing, I would not advise anyone to emulate Weber's style. As stated previously, Pete cultivated this manner of bowling out of necessity. His enormous talent in other aspects of the game more than compensated for his semicontrolled swing. And, despite the fact that several other PBA stars have performed successful semicontrolled armswings, it is far more beneficial to use a free-flowing swing that is coordinated with the first step of a four-step approach or the second step of a five-step delivery.

Controlled Armswing

Few bowlers have achieved greatness with fully controlled armswings. This style of armswing is controlled entirely throughout the pushaway

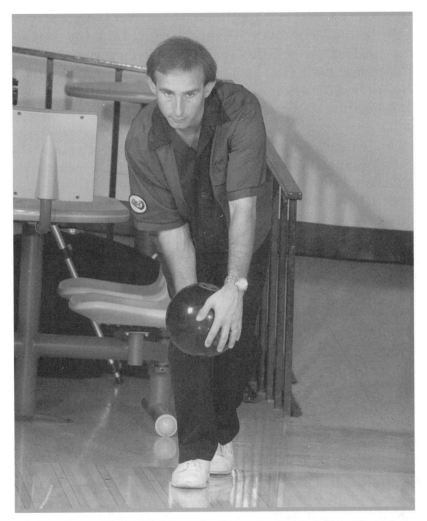

Figure 3.5 Although a free swing is recommended, Norm Duke has been successful using a fully controlled armswing.

to the downswing to the backswing and to the forward swing. (See figure 3.5.) It is employed with full muscle control and appears robotic.

Jim Godman, one of the PBA's top players during the '70s, was one of the few successful players to bowl with a controlled armswing. He won 10 PBA titles, including the Firestone Tournament of Champions in 1973. He also carted off the ABC Masters crown in 1971. Godman was as strong as an ox and possessed forearms like those of a blacksmith. His technique was the epitome of the controlled armswing. Pete Couture enjoyed moderate success on the PBA tour using the controlled armswing. Pete currently rates among the elite group of bowlers on the senior tour.

On the contemporary scene, one of the top players using a muscled armswing is Mike Miller. Miller has established a wide reputation in bowling circles by exercising a thumbless delivery. His inserts his fingers in the ball, which leaves the thumb supporting the weight of the ball, thus creating the necessity for a controlled armswing. He resorted to this uncanny method of execution as a matter of necessity. His inability to apply sufficient revolutions to his ball in a conventional manner compelled him to convert to a technique that would produce better results.

Miller joined the tour in 1980. He bowled in 132 tournaments through 1990 and won a total of $92,691. Beginning the 1991 season, desperate and on the verge of retiring from the tour, Mike decided to convert to a no-thumb delivery. The results were astounding. His strike ball became one of the most potent on tour and Miller experienced instant success. He captured the prestigious PBA National Championship in Toledo and finished the year with total earnings of $99,663, which was $7,000 more than he earned in his previous 10 years on tour. He amassed two other titles: one at Wichita in 1992, another at Dallas in 1999. Muscled armswings are not high on my list of recommendations. However, there is one circumstance that favors this type of delivery. With a bent-elbow backswing, the hand is lodged to remain under the ball in a more effective position. This permits the shot to get greater thrust from the back and inside of the hand, which subsequently provides additional rotation and drive.

The greatest disadvantage of a muscled swing is the physical strain involved. Controlling a ball from the pushaway to the backswing and then through the forward swing requires inordinate strength and can injure the hand, arm, and shoulder. It is also far more difficult to generate speed without sacrificing accuracy. An armswing that is propelled by force cannot match the consistency of a muscle-free swing.

Bob Vespi and Bob Benoit, both now retired, exemplified the fully controlled armswing. Both players cupped the ball, bent their elbows slightly into short backswings, and forced the forward swing through a muscled forearm. A cupped delivery is similar to a thumbless delivery and places extreme pressure on the hand and forearm. If you do not have the arm strength of Jim Godman, bowling in this fashion will inevitably take its toll and prove injurious. Not too surprising, it disrupted Vespi's career and forced him to alter his method of execution. It also took a toll on Mike Miller in the early segment of the 2001 PBA tour. The tremendous strain on Miller's knees forced him out of competition and necessitated surgery.

Bowlers have achieved stardom by using diverse styles and techniques: free armswings, semicontrolled armswings, and fully controlled

Perfecting the Armswing

Mistakes	Modifications
1. Forearm muscles are flexed.	**1.** Relax the arm.
2. Backswing is muscle-pulled.	**2.** Use a soft upward pushaway to create gravity for a free fall of the ball.
3. Swing bumps out (moves right of the hips in the backswing).	**3.** Realign bump-out swing by pushing away slightly to the right.
4. Swing wraps around (moves to the left of the hips in the backswing).	**4.** Realign wraparound swing by pushing the ball away slightly to the left.
5. Downswing is forced.	**5.** Permit ball to descend on its own weight through gravity. Also, try to maintain the ball directly behind your elbow in the downswing until it reaches the flat plane of the forward swing.

armswings. The world is replete with athletes who attained stardom despite the fact that they performed in less-than-textbook fashion.

As I've said all along, and as I've seen in 60 years of observing the best bowlers in the world, a relaxed, free armswing is ideal for maximum effectiveness and continuity in your game. Are there instances when I recommend anything else? No. Although I recognize other unconventional styles and the benefits from some other methods, experience has proven that the free armswing remains the standard of excellence.

Finding a Rhythm Through the Step Sequence

The approach in bowling is like the movement in ballet: smooth, graceful, and naturally synchronized. It is the determining factor in maintaining a free armswing, proper balance, precise position for release, and a fluid follow-through. The approach is the catalyst for setting up quality shots with undue strain or exertion. When you become secure in your approach, your confidence enables you to bowl consistently, shot after shot, game after game.

The trademark of dozens of legendary bowlers is a rhythmic approach. Sheer power and dynamic strike balls are exciting, but the majority of top-rated players rely on perfect timing, finesse, and free armswings to ensure success. The list of bowlers who mastered an ideal approach includes Earl Anthony, Tom Hennessey, George Pappas, and Dick Ritger. Current PBA stars Mike Aulby, Dave Husted, David Ozio, and Brian Voss have achieved tremendous success by blending exact timing with average finger rotation. Power bowlers use a more unnatural and vigorous finger rotation. Although these bowlers perform in an effortless manner, they personify textbook strokers who have taken advantage of modern bowling balls that explode on contact with the pins.

The approach consists of several elements:

☒ The number of steps taken

☒ The length and rhythm of each step

☒ The knee bend

☒ The power step

☒ The slide

The following section discusses each part in detail.

Number of Steps

Most players excel using four- and five-step approaches. Some use six or even seven steps. How many steps make the most fitting approach? Simply put, whatever feels comfortable. The number of steps for an ideal approach is not etched in stone.

Three-Step Approach

The three-step approach is not common, but believe it or not, one of the greatest bowlers in history used three steps. Lee Jouglard, an ABC Hall of Fame member, took only three steps. He not only captured the first ABC Masters title in 1951, but he also set an ABC singles record of 775, a record that stood for 29 years before it was toppled by Mike Eaton at Louisville in 1980.

The pushaway in a three-step approach is initiated with the first step off the left foot (right foot for left-handers) and is quicker than in other walking patterns. The three-step approach relies on a free swing because of the importance of the force created by the weight of the ball. This force is so important because a three-step approach does not provide as much momentum as when four or five steps are taken.

The three-step approach offers no benefit whatsoever to a quality game. Most of all, it is practically void of rhythm. A three-step approach places the ball into the pushaway before the feet move. More often than not, this abnormal method of ball placement produces an undesirable tilt in the pushaway and causes hastier footwork, which disrupts timing.

To my knowledge, no one on the PBA tour employs the three-step approach anymore. Nonetheless, elderly participants, bowlers with slight handicaps, smaller people, and youngsters in junior leagues use the three-step approach occasionally because they lack the ability to consistently coordinate a weighted object with a well-paced approach.

Four-Step Approach

Mike Aulby and Parker Bohn III have earned a place in the PBA Hall of Fame by using four-step approaches. Aulby and Bohn have a lot in common. Both are left-handed. Aulby surpassed the $2 million mark, and Bohn isn't far behind. Both have balletic approaches that flow to the foul line in perfect rhythm. Both have been recipients of the Steve Nagy Sportsmanship Award and both are in the PBA Hall of Fame. Aulby is in the ABC Hall of Fame; Bohn is a virtual cinch when he becomes eligible. Both have over 26 titles and both heeded my advice by reverting to four-step approaches.

I had coaching sessions with Bohn during his early years on tour in the mid-'80s, sometimes until the wee hours of the morning. One of my first recommendations was a four-step approach. Since then, Parker Bohn III has become one of the most fluid players in the game. As soon as Mike Aulby converted to a four-step approach (figure 4.1), he too established himself as one of the smoothest bowlers on the PBA tour.

An ideal four-step approach coordinates the armswing with the footwork to act as a piston: One force propels the other in undeterred cadence. The definitive course for precise rhythm is the coordination of the first step in a four-step approach. A four-step approach eliminates any additional moves that can hinder a bowler's rhythm. I have strongly advocated a four-step approach to professionals as well as amateurs who were plagued by timing problems in five- and six-step approaches. Although some players I coached did not switch exclusively to a four-step approach, they rehearsed this method repeatedly to regain rhythm and timing. You can accomplish this by pushing away on the first step repetitively until the movement becomes natural.

The four-step approach is the standard by which all approaches are measured. In all other approaches the pushaway for a proper approach *must* begin with the first of the last four steps. The majority of qualified coaches recommend four-step approaches for beginner bowlers, and understandably so. Because of its simplicity, it is the most prudent method for developing rhythm and timing. As previously stated, the principal requirement for a proper four-step approach is the simultaneous movement of the right arm and right leg on the first step in the pushaway (opposite for left-handers). This is the beginning of alternating movements of the arms and legs in rhythm.

A four-step approach works best through a free armswing, wherein the arms and legs react as pistons, one propelling the other. That is, in a four-step delivery, if the pushaway coordinates with the first step, the movement and weight of the ball will develop the proper rhythm. To develop a smooth, rhythmic four-step approach, initiate a pushaway with a short first step as stated earlier (figure 4.1a). At this point, the ball should be suspended beyond the first step, a position that permits the ball to drop through gravity. Without hesitation, proceed into the second step (figure 4.1b) and continue your approach with the weight of the ball dictating the cadence and flow of the ensuing steps (figures 4.1, c and d). It is extremely important to keep your footwork gentle and paced to conform with the swing.

To sum up the four-step approach, the first step should be shorter than the length of your outstretched arm. The second step should increase in length from the first step. The third step should be short and quick leading you into the fourth step.

Figure 4.1 Left-hander Mike Aulby demonstrates the ideal four-step approach: *(a)* The first step is shorter than the length of the outstretched arm; *(b)* the second step increases in length from the first step; and *(c)* the third step is short and quick, leading into *(d)* the fourth step.

Five-Step Approach

A five-step approach is identical to a four-step approach, with one important exception. To develop timing for a five-step approach, you must pause slightly after the first step. (See figure 4.2, a-e.) Do *not* apply any movement in the pushaway until the first step has been firmly planted on the approach. In this manner, you are positioned to trigger the pushaway precisely with the second step.

The slight pause will prevent any early movement of the ball before the second step. A premature movement in the pushaway will produce an early swing and influence a release beyond the desired leverage point, a flaw that is as detrimental as a late swing, if not worse. A bowler can compensate for a late swing by merely waiting for the ball to reach the release point. In an early swing, there is no room for adjustment. Some of the greatest players in the game, Bill Lillard, Carmen Salvino, Harry Smith, and Pete Tountas, all ABC Hall of Famers, were successful at

planting early and waiting for the ball. Conversely, early swings cannot be regulated in releases beyond the leverage point. This type of release is described in bowling jargon as *hitting up* on the ball, an absolute no-no.

Earl Anthony, the all-time leading PBA titlist, epitomized the model five-step approach. He floated to the line and executed from a firm, balanced position. Unlike power players, Anthony relied on finesse, an automatic release, and deadly accuracy.

Tim Criss, Dave Husted, David Ozio, and Brian Voss head a group of five-step "tweeners," a term reserved for players who are categorized as neither power nor straight players. In essence, they are power strokers, which means they apply fewer revolutions on the ball than do power players. They are finesse players and forsake sheer power for balance and accuracy.

Walter Ray Williams employs a five-step approach. Williams, whose precision and hand-eye coordination have earned him 30-plus PBA titles and a half-dozen World Horseshoe Pitching Championships, is a rarity

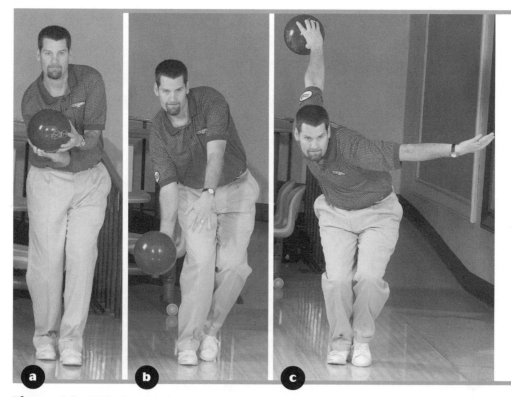

Figure 4.2 Right-hander Dave Husted demonstrates the model five-step approach: *(a)* He pauses slightly after the first step before *(b)* triggering the pushaway and downswing with the second step, then maintains a smooth rhythm in the *(c)* third, *(d)* fourth, and *(e)* fifth steps.

among PBA players. He is neither a power player nor a stroker. He is a straight player with an uncanny release featuring an end-over-end roll, delivered with varied speeds and a thunderous follow-through. His five-step approach displays rhythm and timing. Although his aggressive follow-through results in his rearing up at the line, he is able to maintain accuracy. He is rarely off target and is one of the deadliest spare shooters in the game.

Although most PBA bowlers prefer a five-step approach, some of the top stars have established reputations using six and seven steps. During the '70s and '80s, bowling fans marveled at Mark Roth's six- to seven-step approach. Roth was honored as one of the 20 greatest players of the 20th century. Like Lillard and several other older stars, Roth generates incredible power from a planted slide. Norm Duke, regarded by many of his fellow pros as the most versatile shotmaker on tour, takes five to six small steps but, unlike Roth, Duke relies on hand position, speed control, accuracy, and finesse rather than raw power.

Despite the success of bowlers who use five or more steps in their approaches, I recommend four-step approaches. With a four-step approach you can simultaneously activate the pushaway and the first step much more effectively than you can by applying an extra step. If you're a right-hander, simply start the pushaway on the right foot (left for left-handers). Any movement before the pushaway step is excessive and requires precise timing. Any premature movement or delay leading into the pushaway step will cause a lack of rhythm in the approach. After more than 50 years of close observation of many of the greatest players in the game, I have learned that bowlers using more than four steps encounter greater difficulty in shaking slumps than those who embrace the four-step approach. As in any other sport, fewer and simpler motions provide the greatest chance for success.

Bowlers who use five-step approaches for additional speed can achieve this with a four-step approach by raising the starting position of the ball. This ploy will elevate the backswing and automatically accelerate the forward swing.

Length of Steps

The following guidelines apply to the four-step approach (use opposite instructions if you're a left-hander):

• **First step**—In a four-step approach, the first step should be shorter than the extended point of the arm in the pushaway. This means that any step beyond the extension of the pushaway will impede the free fall of the ball in the downswing. Your body weight must be above your feet, *but* to use gravitational force, the weight of the ball must be beyond the first step.

Consequently, a short first step becomes the catalyst for a free armswing. Steps should be in heel-toe order; that is, the heel makes contact with the approach, followed by the toe, in a natural walking step.

• **Second step**—The second step should increase in length. As the ball descends from the pushaway, pull and extend the left hand back and away, forming an airplane wing. This acts as a counterbalance and maintains the shoulders and body in line with the intended direction of the delivery. At this juncture, the ball should be at the bottom of the pushaway, slightly past the knee, and primed for its path into the backswing.

Del Warren's Successful Transition to a Four-Step Approach

Photo courtesy of Bowling Headquarters, Greendale, WI

Del Warren, now retired from the PBA tour, was one of my pet projects. A 6-foot 5-inch bowler, Warren began his PBA career using a five-step approach. He began his stance at the back end of the approach and took five *giant* robotic steps, completely devoid of rhythm. His backswing soared two feet above his head and his bump-out armswing, which veered off to the right in the backswing, left a lot to be desired.

Del sought my advice and became one of the most willing students I ever had. I began by moving his starting position from the back of the approach to the first set of dots and converted him into a four-step bowler. Can you imagine his shock? He was forced to move his long body up about one-fourth the distance on the approach and change from five long steps to four short, delicate steps. Then he was expected to slide behind the foul line. Warren has long arms and legs, and this transition gave him a cramped feeling. We began our practice session by lowering the ball position in his stance to lower his backswing. We practiced a softer pushaway whereby he was able to transfer the ball weight from the hand to the shoulder. I placed my fingers at his shoulder joint, set my palm slightly higher than his ball placement, and asked him to push the ball up to my palm gently. At this point, I told him to relax all his muscles and let gravity carry the ball into the backswing. We repeated this procedure without taking any steps until Warren could sense a loose, free armswing. We initiated his approach by shortening his first step simultaneously with his pushaway, then proceeded into the approach. With his arms and legs performing in pistonlike fashion, Warren's approach became smooth. Warren became one of the most improved players on the PBA tour. His ball placement and pushaway, combined with a freed-up armswing and a rhythmic approach, converted him from a journeyman player into a legitimate contender. In addition to earning a spot among the top five finalists in the prestigious Firestone Tournament of Champions in 1986, Del succeeded in capturing two titles before retiring from the PBA tour to accept a position with AMF.

Note that many contemporary players, particularly those who employ the power game, extend their nonbowling arms forward, thereby opening their shoulders for "loading up" their release. They usually drift leftward with open shoulders, then realign to the target before releasing the ball. (This will be addressed in chapter 9.)

• **Third step**—Most instruction books suggest increased lengths after the first step, throughout the approach. At the risk of agitating highly regarded instructors, many of whom are my friends, I am opposed to this philosophy. Although the third step is generally acknowledged as the *power step*, it is also referred to as the *trigger step* or the *push-off step*. At any rate, all these terms allude to the main objective and importance of the third step. *Power, trigger, push-off* all convey the central notion for initiating a driving force. To accomplish this important maneuver, you *must* make the step short and rapid. It is virtually impossible to push off on a step that is beyond the upper-body position. The primary role of the power step is the beginning of a forceful surge into the slide, which is described later in this chapter.

To achieve the desired surge going into the slide, use a short, rapid third step by simulating a sitting position. A short step allows you to assume a sitting posture that places your third step in a sturdy base to power into the slide. This suggestion is not just based on theory. Short power steps are, and have been, the trademarks of *every* successful player, from older stars like Dick Weber, Don Carter, Don Johnson, and Earl Anthony to modern players like Norm Duke, Mike Aulby, Brian Voss, and Pete Weber. This assertion can be substantiated through PBA tape replays that are available to anyone with dissenting rebuttals.

Knee Bend

The knee bend is an important component of the third step and a vital element of quality shotmaking. There is a great misconception regarding proper knee bend. I can't begin to tell you how many times I have heard someone say, "Bend your knee on your slide." This phrase seems like constructive advice, but it is far more difficult to perform than it is to convey. Doesn't it seem arduous to bend your knee from an erect position with a weighted object in your hand? How can anyone descend to this level abruptly and maintain any semblance of balance? Consequently, if you find it difficult to descend rapidly, you should begin your stance with a slight bend in your knees, gradually descend on the second step, and assume a sitting position on the third (power) step (figure 4.3). You *must* bend the knee. Tilting the body to achieve a low position is counterproductive and will result in rearing up on the release. A proper knee bend is the catalyst for the power step. A well-administered power step can enhance your game in many other ways. It prevents rearing up at the point of delivery and permits a low trajectory of the release. It is especially effective on oily lanes and permits the arm to extend outward instead of upward in the follow-through. In a well-executed delivery, the ball touches down on the lane like a plane on a runway and is seldom heard when it makes contact with the lanes.

Walter Ray Williams uses a knee bend to execute a near-silent delivery. The only sound you detect in his release is the crash of the ball into the pins. Ryan Shafer and Bob Learn have achieved great success with little or no knee bend. Their fortunes can be attributed to their short

Figure 4.3 Brian Voss illustrates proper knee bend in the third step.

stature. They naturally release from a lower position into the lane, a strategy that minimizes the bouncing effect of the ball.

Oily lane conditions create chaos for bowlers who deliver from a high position. A bounce on a well-dressed lane decreases the ball's solid contact with the lane surface and increases deflection in the ball on contact with the pins. Releasing a ball from a low laydown point on oily lanes will decrease skid: The ball will grip the lanes sooner and create a stronger roll. So I recommend a stance with the knees slightly bent. Descend gradually on the second step, then simulate a sitting position on the third step.

Power Step

The power step is a prominent movement in a model approach. Whether you call it a power step, a trigger step, or a push-off step—all phrases that depict a launching point that affords maximum leverage—you must apply it in a refined manner. The concepts of smoothness and force are somewhat contradictory, but a delicate balance between the two factors is necessary for an ideal delivery.

The power step is the third step of a four-step approach or the fourth step of a five-step approach. Just think of it as the step preceding the slide step. One thing is certain: The power step must be short and quick. (See figure 4.1c on page 53.) An even rhythm is important in footwork, but the power step is the only movement that is deliberately shortened to achieve a desired purpose: to create power in a delivery without throwing you off balance. When you deliver a weighted ball from one side of your body to the other, you are prone to imbalance, which other forces must counteract. Moreover, you must accomplish this with the body in motion. Although your arms and legs automatically function in an alternating manner, you must coordinate the steps precisely to create an ideal release point. Unlike the heel-to-toe steps in the first two steps of a four-step approach, the power step is initiated with a strong, deliberate push off the ball of the foot, which thrusts your body into the slide. It creates the force and thrust of the hand, which permits acceleration through the shot without muscling through the forearm. The power step also propels the body into a position to wait for the ball, thus allowing the weight of the ball to be balanced through the swing. This also prevents an early armswing that would force the ball beyond the sliding step. Remember the secrets to a great power step: Make it quick and short, then sit and push off.

Slide

A major manufacturer ran a bowling shoe commercial on ESPN that featured David Ozio. In it, Ozio stressed the significance of bowling shoes in PBA competition. The commercial featured the attachment and removal of four assorted Velcro inserts for soles and heels, providing 16 different combinations for sliding and braking. It was quite appropriate, particularly in view of Ozio's graceful approach. We've all grown to appreciate the fluid movements of such players as Ozio, Parker Bohn III, Dave Husted, and Brian Voss. All possess powerful deliveries with minimum effort.

Bowling buffs were awed by the graceful approaches of performers like Dave Davis, Tom Hennessey, Joe Joseph, and Dick Ritger, stars of the '50s, '60s, and '70s who displayed immaculate form at the foul line. Joe Joseph was perhaps the smoothest bowler in the history of the game. His delivery was so fluid and clean that his ball made no noise when it made contact with the lane.

An ideal slide is initiated on the ball of the foot and terminated on the heel about two inches from the foul line, as shown in figure 4.4. A good slide results in proper balance and prevents strain to the body. However, a smooth slide isn't the only path to effective bowling. For example, witness the success of such ABC Hall of Famers Bill Lillard, Harry Smith, and Pete Tountas. Lillard, possessor of the strongest ball of his era, *never* slid. He braked on his last step, waited for the ball to reach the release point, and then uncorked the most vicious strike ball I have ever seen. Lillard actually wet his heel with a wet towel or with saliva. This is known as *burning rubber,* a bowling term for leaving heel marks on the lanes. It made life difficult for bowlers who relied on smooth approaches. This was not a ploy to psych out opponents but rather Lillard's personal style.

Harry Smith, another super cranker, braked suddenly, hopped slightly to the right, and then ripped the cover off the ball. Smith's game was unconventional but, during his career, he led more qualifying rounds in PBA competition than any other player, including Don Carter, Billy Welu, Dick Weber, and Ray Bluth. Smith netted 10 PBA titles in his career but was probably denied several more because of the original PBA scoring format, in which all qualifying pins were dropped entering match-play competition.

Pete Tountas used a slow, methodical five-step approach in a heel-to-toe method. He actually planted his slide step. Pete waited for the ball

Figure 4.4   Chris Barnes possesses a smooth, balanced slide.

and stroked a powerful strike ball, one that gave him an ABC Masters title and a place in the ABC Hall of Fame. On the contemporary scene, Jess Stayrook has managed to earn a comfortable living on the PBA tour by bowling without a trace of a slide. In fact, to ensure this manner of execution, Stayrook has worn sneakers or a rubber shoe just on the sliding foot.

Although the aforementioned players have succeeded in making their marks in unconventional manners, they are far outnumbered by players who slide in a fluid manner and maintain perfect balance. To negotiate an ideal slide, you must remember this: The slide step does not advocate the heel-to-toe method. A well-executed slide is initiated on the ball of the foot and braked on the heel.

Proper Alignment During the Slide

One basic rule must be followed, regardless of the number of steps taken. The slide step *must* conclude directly in line with the previous step— that is, in line with the third step in a four-step delivery or the fourth step in a five-step approach. Any slide that is to the left of the previous step for right-handed bowlers or to the right of the previous step for left-handers will shift the weight away from the center of the body and create an imbalance. It will also place the release too far away from the ankle and result in loss of leverage. This can also result in a pulled shot. Therefore, the slide step must be in line with the preceding step. This counterbalance averts "falling off" the shot. It also keeps the armswing close to the body and prevents a "flying elbow."

One of the major sliding mistakes made by amateurs and pros alike is in the position of the toe and heel in relation to the target. In an ideal slide, the toe and heel should be aligned directly with the target. Reactive bowling balls have afforded contemporary power players the opportunity to drift leftward on the lane and realign to the targeted area. A quality shot can be delivered in this style, provided the toe of the sliding step and the shoulder are aligned with the desired target area.

Herein lies the key to a quality shot. The toes *must* follow the line of the body. Although accomplished players like Steve Hoskins, Bob Learn, Brian Himmler, and Pete Weber have been successful in applying this technique, they sometimes become victimized in their realignment process, particularly when lane conditions are not too forgiving.

Don Carter was the dominant star of the '60s. He approached the foul line in near-flawless fashion, yet his style was very unconventional. He bowled from a low crouch, applied a muscled pushaway, pulled the ball into the backswing with a bent elbow, and shuffled to the foul line. *But*, he slid with his toes, heel, shoulder, and armswing *all* aligned to his intended target. He was the deadliest clutch bowler of his generation, principally because of his impeccable footwork.

Ray Bluth, an outstanding bowler, demonstrated the essence of proper balance. Bluth, a right-handed bowler, slid with his heel at least one inch inward from his toe. His balanced position resembled a tripod in that all his body weight was evenly distributed over his sliding step.

John Forst is an employee of Kegel Company's expert lane maintenance crew. He is currently responsible for PBA lane conditions as well as lane maintenance procedures at major tournaments around the world. Before his association with Kegel, Forst competed on the PBA circuit for several years and exhibited an explosive strike ball. With the exception

In an ideal slide, the toe and heel should be aligned with the target.

of a doubles title, Forst failed to capture a PBA championship. His failure to reach his potential was due principally to a faulty slide. John's hips were slightly wider than average and, in an effort to create a clearance in the forward swing, he inadvertently swung his body leftward, shifting his heel four or five inches left of his toes. This, in turn, placed his shoulders and toes open four or five inches to the right of the target area, formulating a side armswing that inhibited Forst's efforts at repeating quality shots.

Rick Steelsmith gained worldwide recognition as an amateur at the FIQ tournament in Helsinki, then proceeded to capture the 1987 ABC Masters title at Niagara Falls. He joined the PBA later in 1987 and was a unanimous selection for Rookie of the Year. A shoulder injury took a tremendous toll on his career, but he returned after a two-year layoff and established himself as a major force on the tour. Despite the fact that he is one of the best shotmakers on tour, a minor flaw in his slide has inhibited his success. To a lesser degree than John Forst, Rick occasionally slides with his toes two or three inches inside his heel, an error that results in a side-arm delivery. Although this flaw isn't habitual, it sometimes hampers his ability to repeat quality shots. Rick Steelsmith's 10-pin stands on seemingly quality shots are proportionately higher than those of most PBA players, a statistic that can be attributed to occasional faulty slides.

Straighten Up and Slide Right Drill

Superstars like Parker Bohn III, Brian Voss, Chris Barnes, and Dave Husted subscribe to the ideal approach of "straighten up and slide right"—with toes and shoulders pointed directly toward the target! If you are experiencing difficulty in sliding properly, you can correct this problem by rehearsing simulated slides without the ball, just as I suggested in correcting foot patterns. Take your stance, continue through the approach, then slide and force your heel and toes in the direction you seek. Repeat this drill until it becomes natural. Try to remember my choice advice, "Repetition creates habit."

Baseball players have two options for sliding: head first or feet first. Bowlers have one choice: the body, the shoulders, and the slide must all be directed toward the target!

Power Player's Approach

The textbook version of a four-step approach is this: Walk three steps in a straight line, then slide directly in line with the preceding step. This approach has become a rarity for many players in an era of explosive bowling balls. Today we see more and more bowlers drifting left from 10 to 20 boards. These are the power players who possess incredible hook balls that cover a path from 15 to 20 boards. They enter the pocket at extreme angles and rely on modern balls to increase strike percentage. Power players' system of execution is diametrically opposed to that of textbook bowlers. They push the ball to the left of their bodies, walk away from the swing, and open their shoulders in the last two steps.

They slide anywhere from the 35th to the 40th board, lay the ball down somewhere between the 28th and 33rd board, cross between the 5th and 6th arrow, and send the ball to an area between the 5th and 10th board at the break point. (All points depend on the condition of lane dressing.)

Steve Hoskins, Brian Himmler, and Rudy Kasimakis stand out among those who walk extremely leftward. They open their shoulders when lanes permit them to open up and unleash explosive strike balls. Himmler's five-step approach features a unique, quick-skipping fourth step, triggering an extraordinary high backswing into an extended follow-through from the shoulder joint (figure 4.5). Kasimakis, also a five-step player, has one of the highest backswings on the tour, yet he possesses one of the smoothest approaches and follow-throughs in the game.

Figure 4.5 Power player Brian Himmler *(a)* opens the shoulders and *(b)* unleashes a powerful strike ball.

Perfecting the Approach

Mistakes	Modifications
1. First step is long.	**1.** Make certain you push the ball away beyond the first step. If the step is beyond the pushaway, it will prevent gravity from producing a free armswing.
2. Second step has excessive drift.	**2.** Reduce drift on second step. If the second step drifts too much, it will necessitate opening up the shoulders to enable the arm movement to clear the hips into the backswing. This, in turn, will require you to realign your body to the intended target
3. Third step is too long and too stiff.	**3.** Make the third step short and quick, and try to assume a sitting position. If the third step is too long, it is almost impossible to bend the knee on the third step. The key to a good knee bend in the sliding step is contingent on a deep knee bend in the third step. The simplest method for this exercise is to assume a sitting position and push off into the slide. This not only helps in overcoming the disadvantage of delivering a ball from a high position; it also thrusts the body forward and keeps the ball behind the leverage area primed for acceleration at the release point.
4. Release position is too high on slide step.	**4.** Push off into the slide and make certain the sliding foot is parallel to the prior step, preferably with the sliding toe in line with the target. A major key for a proper slide is keeping the toe aligned with the heel or slightly inside the heel position. A delivery executed with the toe not pointed in the direction of the target will result in a side-arm delivery and, most likely, a pulled shot.

Pete Weber, arguably the greatest talent in the game today, uses a five-step approach. He exercises an extremely high backswing that he developed as a young bowler. Small in stature, he was compelled to add height to his backswing to gain additional speed. He maintained this style and incorporated a smooth five-step approach with a clean, pure release. Weber drifts leftward and opens up the lanes, but unlike other power players, Pete succeeds with unusually slow ball speed.

Dave D'Entremont, Bob Learn, Amleto Monacelli, and Robert Smith all walk in a leftward approach. Despite their inclination to overpower pins with wide-arcing balls, these players are equally adept at overcoming conditions that are not conducive to their normal manner of execution.

Power balls are exciting and impressive. Power players can be dominant on conditions that permit wide-hooking balls to literally carom off the break points and drive into the pocket with incredible force. "Opening up the lanes" does not require pinpoint accuracy but rather affords power bowlers the luxury of playing an *area* rather than a certain board on the lanes. This is not, in any manner, meant as an indictment of power players. Many PBA players have managed to successfully harness their power under demanding conditions. Power bowlers like Couch, Hoskins, Monacelli, and Weber have exhibited their all-around talents, winning championships under any and every lane condition.

The bowling game is fraught with players, pro and amateur, who unleash dynamic strike balls yet have little to show for it. Timing and accuracy are far bigger advantages to bowlers than high-powered missiles that lack the consistency for overall scoring. In many cases, their inability to compete at the highest level can be traced to a lack of proper footwork, timing, and favorable release points.

Although many bowlers drift leftward intentionally, others have developed natural tendencies toward the left. There are several methods for correcting a drift. One is an age-old exercise of rehearsing a foot pattern on the lanes without a ball. Another is to place tape on the lanes in a desired line and repeatedly retrace the line with eyes glued to the tape. Repeat the procedure until it becomes routine.

Proper footwork is important in addressing spares, particularly for power players. While opening up the lanes on strike shots is a power player's forte, it is important that the body and feet be positioned correctly to convert spares. Straighter shots, accuracy, and proper footwork are far more advantageous than drifting left, opening the shoulders, and delivering high-revolving balls at single, two, or three-pin spares. Always remember that accuracy and proper footwork simplify the game.

One-Three Key

Many players use certain keys to attain their goals. I refer to this exercise as the one-three key because it represents the most crucial area of concentration: the strike pocket. The focus here is on the four-step approach. Although many players employ five-step deliveries, all systems can be seen as variations of the four-step approach. The "one" of the one-three key, the first step of the approach, is important because it is the basic element for a smooth, fluid, and rhythmic approach and a principal factor in a free armswing. The step must be short enough to permit the ball to fall by way of gravity during the pushaway. (See figure 4.1a on page 52.)

You can refine your technique by studying the armswings of top professionals who have developed enviable swings through perfecting their first steps and pushaways. Aspiring bowlers should study pushaways of players such as Mike Aulby, Parker Bohn III, Dave Husted, and David Ozio. They all share one primary fundamental: great pushaway steps, regardless of the number of steps taken in the approach.

Five-step players should pause slightly after the first step to synchronize the pushaway with the second step. (See figure 4.2a on page 54.) This has been the trademark of many great players from the St. Louis area, such as Ray Bluth, Nelson Burton Jr., Dick Weber, and Pete Weber.

The "three" of the one-three key refers to the third step of the four-step approach, commonly referred to as the power step. It is one of the most important elements of a powerful release. Think of the third step as the thrust of a plane from an aircraft carrier or, perhaps, the "turn" in golf (the part of a golfer's swing in which acceleration at the explosion point requires the weight to be shifted from one leg to the other. This is where a golfer generates the power for driving the ball farther).

The third step must be short enough to push off and power into the shot. (See figure 4.1c on page 53.) You can simplify this by taking a longer second step that will enable you to greatly reduce the length of the third step in rapid motion. It must be short enough to permit you to assume a sitting position, which you can facilitate by gradually bending the second step. It is extremely difficult to apply knee bend in the sliding step if the preceding step is erect or less than fully bent.

The shortening of the third step can eliminate "rearing up," a flaw that results in releasing the ball from a high position, causing the ball to bounce rather than be fed into the lanes from a low post. The ball should enter the lane as if it were a plane landing on the runway or a

69

flat rock skipping across the surface of a pond or river. An ideal release is one that is devoid of a "thud" or bounce. Released correctly, the ball merely flows smoothly through the head part of the lane. A short third step permits a bowler to generate tremendous thrust into the last step. A long third step poses great difficulty for assuming a sitting position.

Study some of the pros. Notice that players with the most powerful deliveries take extremely short power steps. This is particularly evident in Marshall Holman's incredible release. Holman's power step is barely beyond the preceding step.

Also, if you are to generate any leverage or power, your release point must be behind the toe. Your thumb must clear the ball by the time it is perpendicular to or slightly behind the shoulder joint, just before reaching the ankle area. The thrust generated by a properly executed third step, which propels the body forward, will permit your hand to remain well behind your ankle joint before it accelerates and applies the necessary action for a powerful release.

Power is the effectiveness of the delivery to carry out the 5-pin with the ball. You can attain this important phase of the game by perfecting your approach, particularly in the first and third steps.

In summary, executing quality shots is a combination of a relaxed swing, a rhythmic approach, a deep knee bend that cultivates a strong power step, and a smooth slide.

5

Releasing the Ball in Perfect Position

One of the most desired aspects for sound bowling execution is a good release. A good release is contingent on the ball's placement well back in the hand. At the release point, the thumb exits quickly, the weight of the ball is then transferred to the fingers, and the fingers project the ball into the lane.

Hand Positions

A leading American insurance company's slogan is "the good hands people." Bowling has its share of good hands people: those who have accomplished the art of changing hand positions to achieve maximum hook, medium hook, and end-over-end roll; to straighten out a shot, or to throw a back-up ball. Proper hand position is the most significant factor in overcoming changing lane conditions.

Many PBA bowlers rely on speed and spin to overcome diverse lane maintenance patterns. Although this philosophy may be successful for some bowlers, those who possess the art of alternating hand positions enjoy a distinct advantage over those with limited skills.

Not too surprising, three of the greatest exponents of superior hand positions, Norm Duke, Mark Williams, and David Ozio, honed their skills through grueling match-game competition in Texas. Duke's versatility can be credited to his innate ability to alter hand positions at any given opportunity. Chris Barnes' meteoric rise to stardom can also be attributed to his mastery of various hand positions. Earl Anthony was masterful at changing hand positions and speed. Mike Aulby, like Anthony, does not rely on an overpowering strike ball. Yet he compensates for this by applying proper hand position, changing speeds, and accuracy.

Figure 5.1 illustrates the major paths to the one-three pocket for right-handers (one-two for left-handers):

☒ Straight ball

☒ Back-up ball (reverse hook)

☒ End-over-end roll

☒ Wide hook

☒ Sharp hook

The following sections describe the hand positions necessary for creating these different shots. Instructions are presented for right-handed bowlers; left-handers need only reverse the instructions.

Straight Ball

Beginners normally throw straight balls, and the smartest professionals utilize a straight shot for converting single pins, particularly 10-pin and 7-pin spares. It's agonizing to watch top-rated bowlers throw wide-arcing balls at single pins. This has been an Achilles heel for a number of PBA players, particularly when addressing single corner pins.

The proper location of the fingers for straight balls is at a 6 o'clock position (figure 5.2 on page 75). The wrist should be broken back and the ball triggered with the two middle fingers driving straight through to the 12 o'clock position with no finger rotation whatsoever. Any finger direction other than straight through will radically affect the movement of the ball. A turn to the right will create a side roll that forces a leftward movement of the ball. Finger rotation to the left will affect the ball in the opposite manner.

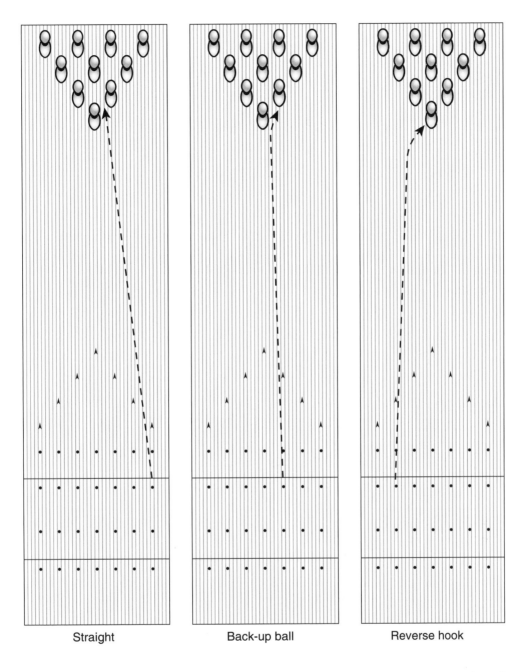

Straight　　　　　　　Back-up ball　　　　　　Reverse hook

(continued)

Figure 5.1 The paths to the pocket.

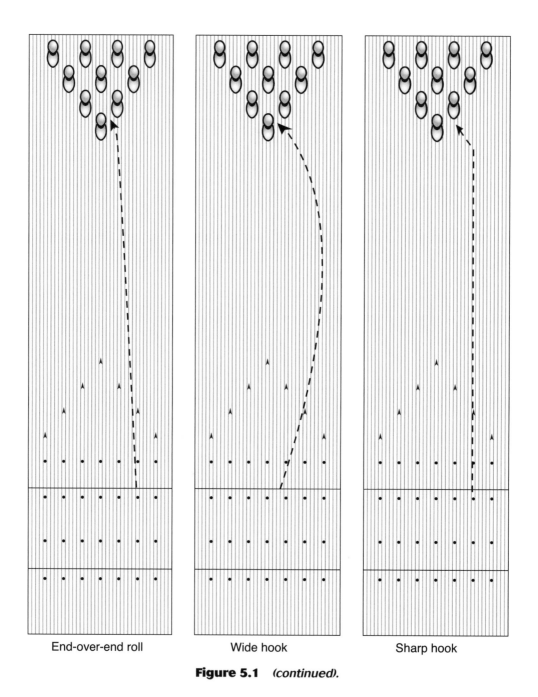

End-over-end roll   Wide hook   Sharp hook

Figure 5.1 *(continued).*

74

A straight ball can be delivered in two ways: As the thumb exits the ball, the fingers do not rotate. Or, as the thumb exits the ball, the fingers rotate over the top of the ball, thus creating a spinning motion in its path to the pocket. This is referred to as a *spinner* and is susceptible to deflection on contact with the pins. Because of the deflection factor, this type of ball lacks the necessary drive into the pins and requires unerring accuracy for high-percentage strikes.

Straight balls have become more useful for safety measures when counts of six or more pins are needed to ensure victory. The straight hard shot has become even more significant after Del Ballard Jr.'s ill-fated gutter shot on a fill ball that cost the burly Texan a championship against Pete Weber several years ago. Ballard needed six pins in the 10th frame to clinch a win. Instead of playing it safe by throwing it down the middle hard and straight, he chose to play the extreme outside angle that had given him the comfortable lead. But the ball fell into the gutter. The horrendous result gave birth to the straight hard delivery that PBA players now implement when counts of six or seven are necessary.

Figure 5.2 Hand position used to deliver a straight ball.

The PBA tour features several players who are considered straight players. However, straight in pro ranks is not akin to throwing the ball completely straight but rather to assuming a stance farther right on the approach and directing the ball in a straighter path to the pocket. Roger Bowker, Michael Haugen, Ernie Schlegel, Butch Soper, and David Traber fit the category of straight players.

Back-Up Ball

Figure 5.3 Hand position used to deliver a back-up ball.

A back-up ball, also called reverse hook, is one that approaches the pocket in a reverse manner. Instead of hooking into the pocket, it moves away from the pocket, directed as though it were thrown by a left-handed bowler. The backup ball is hardly regarded as a strike ball except by beginners who lack proper instruction. Yet some of the PBA's top stars have effectively used this type of delivery. Norm Duke has mastered this shot for 10-pin conversions, and many players use a back-up ball when confronted with the dreaded 2-8-10 split. Mark Williams, one of the most proficient pros in the art of hand control, has had mild success in converting this split, considering the extreme difficulty required for this conversion.

The back-up delivery begins with the fingers anywhere from the 3 o'clock to 6 o'clock position. At the point of release, the hand rotates slightly clockwise (figure 5.3), rolling the ball from left to right. This type of delivery is recommended for proficient and experienced bowlers who apply this high-percentage shot at 10-pins or baby splits.

The reverse hook has become obsolete. A few players practiced it in the '40s, '50s, and '60s. Unlike bowlers who threw back-up balls at 10-pins or baby splits, they stood on the left side of the lane and used it as their strike shot. Reverse-hook bowlers applied extraordinary finger rotation from approximately a 5 o'clock position to an 11 or 12 o'clock position. The drive and path of the ball were very similar to those delivered by left-handed players and, unlike back-up balls that deflect, reverse hooks maintained enough drive to carry through the pocket with efficient force. Ernie Hoestery, a standout player from New England, averaged between 200 and 210 in an era when only the most elite bowlers recorded 200 averages.

End-Over-End Roll

The end-over-end roll is the simplest shot for controlling the ball's path to the pocket. It has a great strike percentage and, although it lacks the thunderous impact of a hard-hooking ball, it possesses enough rotation to carry out the 5-pin. The greatest disadvantage in this delivery is its tendency to leave occasional weak 10-pins, particularly when back-ends inhibit the added rotation required for maximum carry. However, this is balanced by its effectiveness in blowing out 4-pins and 7-pins. Furthermore, an end-over-end roll is less inclined to leave a 9-pin. In this age of reactive and Proactive bowling balls, 9-pins (8-pins for lefties) have become increasingly visible on strong pocket hits for right-handers.

Walter Ray Williams has demonstrated an incredible ability to repeatedly place the ball in the pocket with an end-over-end roll. Williams possesses one of the highest strike percentages on the PBA tour and rarely leaves more than two pins on any shot. Williams' Achilles heel is his occasional

Figure 5.4   Hand position used to deliver an end-over-end roll.

penchant to stray from his strong suit (end-over-end roll) and attempt to compete with the "big hookers." But, overall, he is the most dominant player in the game, all because of his mastery of the end-over-end roll.

The end-over-end roll is one of the most effective deliveries for extreme outside lines with soft back ends. David Ozio has made a career using the end-over-end delivery on "gutter shots" (that is, extreme outside angles).

For an end-over-end roll, the fingers are at the 6 o'clock position before the release (figure 5.4). The wrist is straight; the ball is nested in the palm of the hand and rolled in a straightforward motion. The rotation of the ball must be generated from the *middle finger* to minimize side roll. The release must be completely free of any ring-finger turn. Any application of the ring finger in the release will be counterproductive and create undesired side roll. A modified version of the end-over-end ball is known as a *curve ball*. The curve ball requires a *slow* rotation of the *middle* finger from the 6 o'clock position to approximately a 4 or 5 o'clock position. The speed is slower and the path of the ball is wider. It is more difficult to control but is advantageous on slicker surfaces. This is due to minimum spin and slower speed that tends to create more friction on the lanes.

Wide Hook

I affectionately term the wide-sweeping hook as the *Hollywood shot* for its flash and exhilaration. Wide-sweeping hooks that cover 20 to 25

Pete Weber has done well using the wide-sweeping hook.

boards, or roughly 50 to 60 percent of the lane, create excitement and demonstrate raw power. Bowlers with this type of delivery can be equated to baseball hitters who blast horsehides into outer space, even though their statistics may not be impressive at the end of the season.

Nonetheless, all-time greats Bill Lillard, Junie McMahon, and Carmen Salvino (before altering his game) bowled their way into halls of fame with wide-sweeping hooks. On the current scene, Pete Weber, Robert Smith, Dave D'Entremont, and Brian Himmler have done very well with wide-sweeping hooks. Although these players demonstrate tremendous hitting power, they also symbolize the old adage of "You live and die by the sword." For example, in contrast to the successful bowlers just mentioned, former PBA players Kelly Coffman, Bob Vespi, Scott Alexander, and Bob Spaulding, great exponents of wide-arcing shots, have all departed from the PBA tour, principally because they were unable to control their deliveries on spare shots.

The wide hook is undoubtedly the most potent, most vigorous of all deliveries for pin-carry potential. Conversely, it can result in the most bizarre spares imaginable, particularly on conditions played from outside angles. Grotesque splits like the 2-8-10, the 2-4-6-7-10, and occasionally the 1-2-3-4-5-7-8-10 splits have emerged since the advent of reactive urethane bowling balls.

The wide hook is executed in direct contrast to the end-over-end release. Finger rotation is paramount. In fact, fingers are positioned at 10 to 11 o'clock, rotating approximately two-thirds of a complete circle around the ball; the thumb never ends beyond the 12 o'clock point. (See figure 5.5.) The thumb *must* clear the ball before it reaches the toe and the weight of the ball is transferred to the fingers. Before the release, the ring finger should be at about 11 o'clock and all rotation

Figure 5.5 Hand position used to deliver a wide hook.

generated by the fingers only. Again, the thumb position should never rotate beyond the 12 o'clock point. Ideally, it should end up at 12 o'clock to dissuade overspin.

The overwhelming advantage of sweeping-hook balls is the tremendous power generated in the delivery. Wide-hooking balls afford a greater pocket entry angle and are far more explosive at pin impact. Also, this type of delivery requires far less precision than lesser-hooking balls. In fact, these shots are not contingent on targeting certain boards but, more or less, on an area of the lane.

On the other hand, the greatest drawback of wide-sweeping hooks is the difficulty in controlling the ball movement. Although there are exceptions to the rule, most bowlers using this type of game are condition bowlers; that is, lane maintenance plays an important role in their performance. For example, the majority of proprietors around the country favor high scores. Lanes are dressed with considerable oil on the inside. The last 15 feet of the lanes are bone dry. High-average bowlers merely stand left on the approach, swing the ball out to the six or seven board approximately 45 to 50 feet down the lane, and delight in the sweeping trajectory of the ball as it engages the greater friction of the back ends of the lanes. By virtue of the oil buildup in the one-three area, the ball holds the pocket and this results in a strike. This manner of lane maintenance has produced an unbelievable outbreak of 300 games and 800 series. Additionally, as of this writing, five 900 series have been recorded.

Most lane proprietors endorse high scores as a sensible business ploy. After all, bowlers who post high scores are more content and inclined to return to a bowling center than they would be if they performed poorly. However, this type of lane maintenance has created a rash of gratuitous 220- to 240-average bowlers that do nothing to encourage a more skillful approach to the game. Moreover, these same players become demoralized in tournaments that require quality shots and skillful execution. Again, this is no indictment of skillful bowlers who have mastered the wide hook. Players like Jason Couch (10 titles), Steve Hoskins (10 titles), and Pete Weber (24 titles) have mastered the game with wide-arcing shots, whereas Dave D'Entremont, Robert Smith, Bob Learn, and Ryan Shafer, all multiple champions, have performed exceptionally well throwing wide-sweeping hooks. Although Jeff Lizzi and Jason Hurd have not quite achieved their potential, they have more than held their own on the PBA tour by using wider-than-average hook shots.

Sharp Hook

A sharp hook is the safest and soundest delivery for effective scoring. It incorporates power and accuracy, and, although it does not have the tremendous hitting effect of a wide-sweeping hook, it is far easier to control and is less susceptible to difficult spare shots. The sharp hook was the trademark for such Hall of Famers as Don Carter, Ray Bluth, and Buddy Bomar. David Ozio, Brian Voss, and David Husted, three of the steadiest and most accurate bowlers on the PBA tour, are also exponents of the sharp hook. They have carved very successful careers using this type of delivery.

The position of the fingers for a sharp hook is similar to that of a wide hook, with one exception. Players who rely on wide hooks place their fingers farther under the ball, at approximately 10 or 11 o'clock, and rotate to 3 o'clock. Sharp hooks are performed with fingers at 6 or 7 o'clock (figure 5.6a) and rotated to 3 o'clock (figure 5.6b). Bowlers who

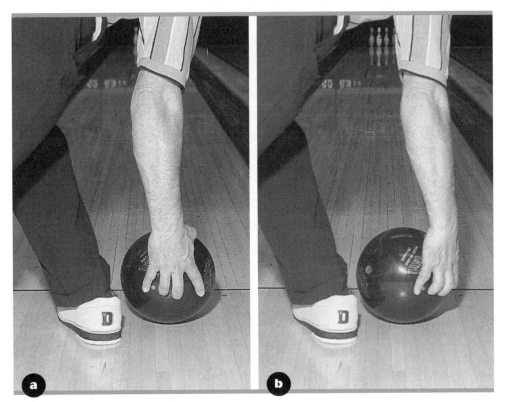

Figure 5.6 In a sharp hook, the fingers start at *(a)* 6 or 7 o'clock and rotate to *(b)* 3 o'clock.

81

deliver sharp hooks cover far fewer boards and display greater accuracy, which generally makes them superior spare shooters.

Release Point

A great release is the envy of every bowler who is not blessed with this God-given talent. I will address the ideal release later in this chapter because an ideal release is ineffective, actually worthless, if not executed at the proper release point.

What is the release point and why is it important? An ideal release point affords an opportunity to launch the ball out on the lane from its strongest leverage area. This is one of the most important elements for consistent scoring. It is also one of the most difficult flaws for bowlers to detect. A faulty release point feels natural and doesn't affect balance; yet the ball reaction is far from effective. The ineffective ball reaction is usually the result of an early swing, where the release point is beyond the leverage area. This is the area that provides the greatest leverage for delivering a quality shot. A great release can be advantageous but can also be unproductive if not executed from a proper release point.

Here is a perfect analogy for determining an ideal release point: Envision a double-ball bag held in line with (or parallel to) the shoulder-ankle line. Lifting weight at this position places little or no stress on the arm and shoulder and affords easy maneuverability. Thus, this becomes the strongest leverage area, yet it maintains proper balance. Likewise, place this same weight slightly behind the shoulder-ankle area. This also affords easy projection on the lane yet retains proper balance. Conversely, if you set the identical load beyond the ankle-shoulder area, the weight of the ball will force the body forward, adversely affect leverage in the shot, and certainly disrupt proper balance.

Preventing Early Swings

During the practice session of the 1999 PBA National Tournament in Toledo, Tim Criss was experiencing difficulty in his ball reaction and sought my help. After a few minutes of observation, I detected his problem. Criss, a five-step bowler, was initiating his pushaway ahead of his second step. This resulted in an early swing that placed his release beyond the strongest leverage point. There are two strategies for executing proper release points and preventing early swings.

1. In a four-step delivery, you can initiate the first step a fraction ahead of the pushaway. In a five-step approach, begin the second step a tad ahead of the pushaway.

2. You can speed up the approach.

Criss is renowned for an unusually slow cadence in his approach so, rather than disrupting his rhythm, I recommended starting his second step slightly before his pushaway. This maneuver delayed his swing long enough to sufficiently place his release behind the ankle, with no appreciable effect on his slow cadence. Incidentally, Tim Criss won the tournament.

Preventing Late Swings

On the other hand, if the swing is late, it indicates a late pushaway and possibly a rushed approach. A late swing will inadvertently result in a forced forward swing (pull) if the armswing isn't loose. Prompting the pushaway or slowing the approach can alter a late swing just as it alters an early swing. Because slowing down the approach is detrimental to good rhythm and timing, I strongly suggest an earlier pushaway to overcome a late swing.

The objective, as stated previously, is to place the release point in its strongest position. Bowlers come in all sizes, so you must take into account the length of your arms and legs to reach a positive point of release. For example, if a release point is beyond the leverage area, this is a sign of an early swing. Early swings can be attributed to two things: a premature pushaway or a slow approach. Therefore, you must take measures to either delay the pushaway or speed up the footwork. You can accomplish this through the process of elimination. Try both methods until you determine the objective in the most comfortable manner.

Release

Hundreds of PBA players, as well as countless high-ranking amateurs, are blessed with great releases. Unfortunately, a great release does not ensure success. Many players display an aura of invincibility. They unleash high-revving missiles that rip the racks but, in numerous cases, they may suffer from faulty armswings, undue force, errant direction, and the inability to control the ball.

Contrary to popular belief, revolutions are not necessarily the key to great strike percentage. Average revs, accurately delivered, are far more effective than wide-arcing shots that cover 15 to 20 boards and enter the pocket from extreme angles. These explosive missiles look awesome as they clear the decks with incredible force, but they may likely leave ringing 10-pins, solid 9-pins, hard 7-pins, occasional 4-pins, and the dreadful 7-10 split. Moreover, when back ends have been altered by oil carry-down, a wide-arcing ball often produces the ugliest of all splits, the 2-8-10. Although a ball with less rotation lacks the hitting power of high-revved missiles, its entry angle can equalize the strike percentage. Rather than execute a power release, this type of bowler—a stroker-type player—performs with a smooth stroke, accuracy, and proper balance. Although a great release is a coveted advantage, it does not ensure stardom.

What constitutes a great release? An ideal release is delivered with the hand well under the ball, the fingers starting anywhere from the 6 o'clock to the 7 o'clock position (figure 5.7). At the release point, a rapid exit of the thumb is a must. The weight is then shifted fully to the fingers, which rotate to the 3 o'clock position. Any rotation of the fingers beyond the 3 o'clock position, or the thumb past 12 o'clock, will create spin instead of roll.

As stated previously, the major disparity between successful bowlers and less successful players is the release point, the point of the downswing that arrives at the flattest plane and affords the strongest leverage opportunity for launching the ball out on the lane. The rapid exit of the thumb is paramount because any ball delivered with the thumb in the ball beyond the sliding foot will result in "hitting up" on the shot— that is, releasing the ball in an upward direction instead of out on the lane. Hitting up destroys the ball's effectiveness in several ways. A ball released in an upward manner is automatically spinning in midair before making contact with the lane. This can result in overreaction, an early hook, and a marked weakness in rotation.

Staying Under the Ball

Staying under the ball is the ability to keep the ball well into the hand with the thumb on the lower side of the ball in cuplike fashion. Bowling manuals have suggested numerous methods for staying under the ball. Some have suggested closing the armpit from the top of the swing to the point of release. Jim Stefanich, one of the all-time greats, placed a towel under his armpit and kept it in this position throughout the

Figure 5.7 Chris Barnes demonstrates an ideal release.

swing. You may favor the Steve Hoskins method of execution of keeping the thumb outside the ball from the top of the swing to the point of release. Or, you may prefer keeping the forearm facing the target from the release point to the follow-through or perhaps keeping the elbow tucked into your side on the downswing.

These methods have been successful for many bowlers, but one fact remains: There are no set patterns. Bowling manuals merely serve as guides for attaining a desired purpose. I do not disprove any of the methods mentioned earlier. Yet, in each case, there is undue strain to the forearm that may conceivably initiate muscle tension and deter the flow of a free armswing.

Helping Marshall Holman Regain His Flawless Release

In 1986, Marshall Holman experienced his first major slump as a PBA player. Bowling at the PBA National in Toledo, Holman shot a most uncharacteristic score of approximately 250 pins under for the 16 games, placing him far down the list of qualifiers. For the first time in his career, Holman was discouraged, seemed lost, and sought my advice. After arranging a workout session at a nearby bowling center, I noticed two flaws in his game. The first was that his hand was out of place at the release point. Holman, whose release was the most envied on tour, was turning his hand too early and releasing off the side of the ball instead of remaining under it, thereby sacrificing all the potential power he normally possessed. Holman had a very short backswing, yet he managed a free forward swing. Therefore, I advised Holman to initiate his forward swing with his ring finger ahead of the rest of his hand. I urged him to maintain this hand position until the last split-second before releasing the ball. After several minutes of continuous execution in this manner, Holman rediscovered his incredible release.

The second flaw was just as serious. Although he reestablished his release, he was sliding away from the shot and losing leverage in the delivery. Holman's slide is much longer than any average player's. In fact, he is the only bowler I've seen on the PBA tour whose slide continued after he released the ball. During our workout, I noticed his slide moving away from the swing line. This is an absolute no-no. The ideal slide must be in direct line with the preceding step to maintain proper balance and maximize leverage. Sliding away from the preceding step places the weight of the ball and body to one side and causes an imbalance. Sliding in under the preceding step forms a tripod. It keeps the ball into the body line and prevents a flying elbow—that is, a forward swing with the elbow outside the swing line and away from the strongest release point. Sliding in under the previous step also distributes the weight of the body evenly for proper balance.

After the correction of these errors, Holman returned for his third qualifying round and shot 300 pins over for the eight-game block. Unfortunately, he was unable to survive the first cut. We continued the workout the following week at Windsor Locks, Connecticut. Although Holman did not win the tournament, he made the finals and headed for the crown jewel of the PBA tour, the Firestone Tournament of Champions. Armed with restoration of his talent and renewed self-assurance, Holman captured the Tournament of Champions for the second time.

Ring-Finger Lead Drill

I devised a method to stay under the ball yet maintain a free armswing. I refer to my system as a *ring-finger lead.* In the ring-finger lead, all movement is initiated from the hand (the lowest and heaviest part of the swing) requiring no muscle tension.

After reaching the top of the backswing, lead the downswing with the ring finger preceding the middle finger until the release point. At this time, the ring finger should be at about a 9 to 10 o'clock position. Then the thumb exits the ball, and the weight of the ball is transferred to the fingers. The fingers then rotate from the bottom to the 3 o'clock position, simultaneously projecting the ball outward on the lane.

Experimenting With Different Releases

Power players such as Pete Weber, Steve Hoskins, Ryan Shafer, Amleto Monacelli, and Robert Smith all begin their hand positions with the fingers at approximately the 9 o'clock position. Power strokers like Mike Aulby, Parker Bohn III, Dave Husted, David Ozio, and Brian Voss initiate their release with fingers at the 6 o'clock position, seldom rotating beyond 3 o'clock.

Danny Wiseman, a pure stroker, is an exception to the rule. He actually begins his hand position in the same manner as power players, yet he strokes the ball gently. Strokers rarely have excessive rotation of the ball. It is important to note that all these players execute with minimum effort and soft, flowing follow-through. Again, a great release is not a guarantee for success. Many players on the regular PBA tour possess this innate talent and have attained incredible success, but an equal number have failed to take advantage of this important element of the game. For example, few bowlers can boast of greater releases than those of Brian LeClair, Paul Koehler, Eugene McCune, or recent retirees from the tour, Kelly Coffman and Joe Firpo. As yet, there isn't a singles title among them.

Several other types of releases have proven very effective. The most notable is the one used by Walter Ray Williams (figure 5.8). Walter Ray defies all odds for proper execution. He releases with extra effort, rears up at the line, and seems off balance. However, he has a rhythmic approach, a loose swing, and the most incredible hand-eye coordination of anyone on tour. These traits earned him six World Horseshoe Championships.

Williams' forte is his ability to keep his hand directly behind the ball. He applies little or no finger rotation, rolls the ball in an end-over-end

87

© Sleeping Dogs Communications

Figure 5.8 Walter Ray Williams' rhythmic approach and deadly accuracy help him overcome a seemingly off-balance release.

rotation, and almost always places the ball in the 1-3 pocket. High-powered reactive urethane balls with sophisticated core configurations have enhanced his strike percentage. His deadly accuracy, coupled with the proliferation of modern explosive equipment, has converted Williams' previously weak 10-pins into strikes.

Butch Soper relies principally on accuracy by using a straighter line to the pocket. He releases with greater spin than do bowlers with average hooks. He accomplishes this by rotating his fingers over the top of

Perfecting the Release

RELEASE POINT

Mistake	Modifications
1. Thumb in ball at release point is beyond ankle, usually because of early swing or very slow feet.	1. Do not place the ball into pushaway before the first step in a four-step approach.
	2. Step gingerly for rhythm. Slow feet tend to disrupt rhythm and timing and induce an early swing. If increasing the cadence of the steps is uncomfortable or doesn't conform to the armswing, it is advisable to start the first step a fraction before the pushaway.

RELEASE

Mistakes	Modifications
1. Wrist is lax.	1. Keep wrist firm.
2. Ball is not nested back into the hand.	2. Place ball well back into the hand, and cup wrist at the top of the backswing.
3. Downswing has an early turn.	3. Lead the downswing with the ring finger.
4. Thumb is in ball too long.	4. Release the thumb at the flat plane of the forward swing *before* the ankle area. Transfer weight of the ball to the fingers and simultaneously accelerate and rotate the fingers and *project* the ball *out* on the lanes. Do not permit the thumb to rotate beyond the 12 o'clock position.

the ball, taking advantage of the increased friction tendered by the reactive advancements made to bowling balls.

Dave Arnold and Ernie Schlegel, like Traber, Bowker, and Soper, also use a straighter path to the pocket, but they apply less spin with more roll. They do not rotate their fingers beyond the 12 o'clock position.

Several players on the PBA tour have experimented with different hand releases that converted them from mediocrity to stardom. Norm Duke is a prime example. Norm was merely a journeyman bowler for many years until he began to experiment with assorted hand positions, different speeds, and different angles. He finally mastered his craft and, since this transformation, he has become a favorite to win every tournament he enters.

"Cup and Collapse" Release

Numerous players on the PBA tour use a technique I call the "cup and collapse" release. Del Ballard heads a list of contemporary bowlers whose deliveries fit this category. (See figure 8.5b on page 126.) Chris Barnes, Paul Koehler, Jeff Lizzi, and veteran Mark Williams also feature this type of delivery.

It can be performed in two manners: using a free swing or a controlled/semi-controlled swing. In a free swing, you place the ball into the pushaway and let it fall into the backswing with its own gravitational force. At the top of the backswing, cup your wrist and maintain this hand position until the release point. Then, collapse your wrist and drive the ball into the lane. This type of release creates a heavy roll and presents great strike potential.

In a controlled "cup and collapse" release, the ball rests back in the palm of the hand at the beginning of the stance. It is drawn back with a bent elbow. The elbow remains bent throughout the swing. At the release point, the wrist collapses and the fingers drive the ball into the lane. Although this is the ultimate method for staying under the ball, it can take a toll on the hand, wrist, and elbow. It can also affect the knees and legs.

A number of PBA players can trace injuries to the strenuous controlled "cup and collapse" release. This method of execution, in great part, curtailed and possibly ended the career of former touring player, Bob Vespi. It also sidelined Mike Miller, whose thumb-less delivery placed severe strain on his wrist and knees.

Many players who have been blessed with great releases have failed to take advantage of this gift. As stated earlier, a great release is not the guarantee for successful bowling. Average releases at ideal release points, accuracy, and balance are the principal ingredients for a top-quality bowling game.

Smoothing Out the Follow-Through

One of the most essential elements of a quality shot in bowling is a sound follow-through. An ideal follow-through is the result of proper execution, balance, accuracy, power, carry percentage, and most of all, consistency. A quality follow-through is delivered with a fully extended arm with minimum arm bend; that is, the projection of the ball is initiated from the shoulder joint, not the elbow. This is the essence of *extension*. In a proper extension, the weight of the swing must be generated from the shoulder throughout the entire swing and follow-through. Any exertion from the elbow is counterproductive. However, the weight of the ball will automatically induce a slight bend of the elbow in the follow-through, *but* bending the elbow to influence power in the shot will destroy the flow of a follow-through. Moreover, it will create undesired ball reaction.

In the current environment, we are witnessing deterioration in the art of proper follow-through. This is primarily due to lane conditions that enable bowlers to merely stand far to the left, swing the ball out toward the gutter, and rejoice as balls bounce off the dry boards and head left into the pocket. Does this sound harsh? Perhaps, but unfortunately, this bold fact is substantiated by many high-average league bowlers' inability to demonstrate their skills on conditions other than those tailored for fictitious scores. What complicates the issue is that bowling ball manufacturers have created equipment that feature sophisticated cores with strategic pin placements surrounded by supercharged urethane covers. Manufacturers have designed balls that increase friction on the lanes. This friction has significantly altered the game by allowing the balls to hook as never before.

Additionally, bowlers who desire to refine their follow-throughs are hard-pressed to sort out the information they seek. The majority of instructional books recommend some or all of the following: Reach for the ceiling, follow through with your hand behind your ear, lift and loft. I have never subscribed to the lift-and-loft philosophy. I even opposed this manner of execution during the era of old rubber balls and shellac surfaces. And now, after observing the greatest bowlers in the world for the past 50 years, I feel confident that these antiquated methods of execution are far more detrimental than beneficial, particularly in the modern bowling environment. This is not meant to demean the techniques recommended by qualified instructors; rather, it is an enforcement of personal beliefs that have proven successful during my coaching career.

Delivering the Ball *Into* the Lane

Before the advent of high-powered urethane balls, it may have been advantageous for some players to subscribe to the lift-and-loft method for releasing the ball, but I have always suggested throwing the ball *into* the lane from a low position. In this manner, the bouncing effect is greatly minimized, and the ball is permitted to proceed uninterrupted on its course. As stated in chapter 4, this is akin to landing a plane. Skillful pilots skim the landing strips and touch down with barely any bouncing effect, thus accomplishing a smooth landing.

I feel secure in my conviction that releasing the ball in an upward trajectory is counterproductive. Conventional wisdom dictates that balls delivered in an upward manner tend to spin in midair before making contact with the lanes. This results in the ball's bouncing, overreacting, and veering off course. In PBA terms, this type of delivery is referred to as *hitting up on the ball*. Releasing balls on the upswing results in weak 10-pins, buckets (2-4-5 for right-handers, 3-5-6 for lefthanders), and abominable splits.

A ball driven into the lane from a low position with a low, outward follow-through will react as a flat rock thrown across a lake does: It skims along unimpeded. To encourage this type of release and follow-through, I created the over and under drill, which was introduced in chapter 3. The over and under drill can also help you execute a fluid follow-through with this addition: After the release, think *low* and *long*.

Low and Long Drill

The "over" phase of chapter 3's over and under drill referred to the *ideal pushaway*. You placed an imaginary bar about waist high and pushed the ball over the bar to create a free armswing. Now, in the second phase of the over and under drill, you place an imaginary bar about 12 inches above the foul line and release the ball under the bar.

After the release of the ball "under the bar," I suggest the substitution of two Ls: *lift* and *loft,* for *low* and *long* (figure 6.1). The low and long system eliminates hitting up.

Figure 6.1 To execute a fluid follow-through, after the release, think *low* and *long.*

Follow-Through Styles of the Pros

Reactive bowling balls have had a profound effect on the modern bowling game. This is particularly noticeable among younger bowlers who are obsessed with wide-arcing balls that rip the racks on light hits. Modern missiles also fascinate players who previously struggled in their efforts to apply sufficient revolutions for carrying percentage. In their desire to deliver powerful strike shots, many average players forego their normal games, exaggerate their follow-through, and rely on reactive bowling balls with strategically placed weights to maximize their scoring potential.

Knowledgeable PBA bowlers also take advantage of ball surfaces, pin placements, and weight block designs. However, the successful bowlers combine this knowledge with proper execution, which culminates in an outward, smooth, extended follow-through with *minimum* arm bend. Many of the more successful PBA players possess this prime ingredient. Veteran bowlers like Mike Aulby, David Ozio, and Brian Voss (figure 6.2) seldom apply excessive effort in following through their shots. Each of them performs in his own style, but all of them conclude their deliveries in a fluid manner: fully extended, with little or no force.

Marshall Holman, one of the most successful players in the history of the PBA, was regarded as a power bowler. Although he possessed a potent strike ball, the "Medford Meteor" had one of the most fluid strokes in the game. His follow-through, generated from a short backswing, was extended in an outward direction. The PBA featured numerous power strokers who bowled their ways into the Hall of Fame. Among them are Dave Davis, Jim Stefanich, Dick Ritger, George Pappas, and Billy Welu.

An aggressive upward follow-through is far less effective than one stroked in an outward direction. Revolutions on a ball are not the result of extraordinary force through the forearm. Revolutions are generated through the fingers, not the arm. Observe the deliveries of Chris Barnes and Robert Smith, two of the PBA's brightest stars. Both players possess unusually potent strike balls and both follow through with arms barely bent, always outward.

Conversely, Pete Weber's follow-through is extremely high yet very effective. This is simply because Pete's arm is fully extended and the delivery is executed from the shoulder instead of the forearm. Weber's high follow-through is principally a result of a high backswing he developed as a youngster. Small in stature, Pete cultivated this style to generate speed and, through the years, mastered this style. Although I

Figure 6.2 Brian Voss executes an ideal follow-through: smooth and extended.

do not recommend Pete's method of bowling, he is certain to land in every hall of fame possible.

Walter Ray Williams stands out among players who use a hard-driving follow-through (figure 6.3). Williams doesn't employ this style to produce more revolutions but rather to generate more speed. Speed is a prime necessity in Walter Ray's game because he relies on an end-over-end roll. He is far less effective when he attempts to abandon his specialty shot and match players who excel on hooking conditions. However, his uncanny hand-eye coordination keeps him fairly competitive

95

Figure 6.3 Although not recommended, Walter Ray Williams has been successful using a hard-driving follow-through.

on dry hooking conditions. Nevertheless, his greatest advantage lies in an end-over-end roll, which is extremely effective with reactive bowling balls but tends to roll out if not delivered with sufficient speed. Consequently, speed is necessary for maintaining power in his shot. That is why Walter Ray uses a vigorous follow-through.

As stated in other chapters, there are no set standards for success. Although a smooth, fluid follow-through is recommended, there are exceptions to the rule. For example, Mark Roth has achieved tremendous success. Mark revolutionized the game in the early '80s by uncorking one of the most thunderous strike balls in bowling history. He placed his fingers in the most extreme manner for maximum turn: at about the 10 or 11 o'clock position. He released the ball with tremendous finger rotation, counterclockwise to the 12 o'clock position. Roth is credited with inspiring and converting thousands of youngsters to this type of game.

Although Roth's follow-through was not textbook, it served him well. Roth garnered 34 PBA titles using one of the most aggressive styles in the history of the game. His thumb at the release point was set at about 5 o'clock. In releasing the ball, Roth applied a wicked snap of the wrist and fingers, then unleashed his trademark devastating strike ball. Unlike textbook bowlers with extended follow-throughs, Roth exerted inordinate force and sported one of the most hideous thumbs imaginable. Although Roth influenced America's youth during the '70s and '80s, I hardly recommend his manner of execution, as it can cause inconsistency and injury due to overexertion.

Many of today's young power players use a fiercely accelerated follow-through. Diminutive Ryan Shafer, the PBA star from Elmira, New York, unleashes one of the most potent strike balls on tour and maintains one of the highest averages among professionals. Unlike softer strokers who follow through in an outward direction, Shafer rips through the ball with excessive force in a skyward direction.

Kelly Coffman, who retired from the PBA tour a few years ago, used a muscle-driven follow-through. Coffman delivered the strongest ball on tour—as many as 24 revolutions. His power was generated through incredible upward motion of the forearm. Despite the crushing effect of his strike ball, Coffman was often victimized by inordinate spares and wide-open splits, which are normal results of wide-arcing balls entering the pocket at extreme angles. This is, by no means, intended to slight numerous power players who exert enormous energy in following through. PBA stars Jason Couch, Brian Himmler, Dave D'Entremont, Jess Stayrook, and Bob Learn all apply firm acceleration in finishing off their shots.

Parker Bohn III, the premier left-hander on the PBA tour, has one of the most fluid armswings in the game. Oddly, he is a rare exception regarding an extended follow-through. Even though he executes his delivery fluidly, he follows through with his elbow bent in a recoil fashion behind his left ear, a rare irregularity among superstars. Steve Jaros, though not as successful as Bohn, also follows through in a recoil manner with his elbow bent behind his ear. Normally, this is counterproductive in today's era of explosive bowling balls, which produce sharp-hooking, often uncontrollable balls plagued by overreaction.

Correcting the Follow-Through Styles of Steve Hoskins, Amleto Monacelli, and Tim Criss

Tim Criss

Steve Hoskins joined the PBA tour in 1989. Like many of the aforementioned players, he exerted excessive force in his follow-through. Although he was elected Rookie of the Year, he was rather erratic in spare conversions and failed to emerge victorious in his first three years on tour.

He sought my advice in 1993. My first objective was a strategy to temper his follow-through. We started by suppressing his forearm thrust and emphasizing a greater swing from the shoulder. Without sacrificing any power, he softened his delivery slightly, eliminated a major portion of his forearm action, and completed his follow-through with his arm fully extended outward. Two weeks later, Hoskins notched his first PBA title at Grand Prairie, Texas. Since then, he has annexed nine additional titles, placing him in the elite 10-title fraternity.

Amleto Monacelli has recorded 18 titles and 33 perfect games to date. He has earned more than $1.8 million in his career and gained most of his fame before the advent of reactive bowling balls. Amleto was one of few successful players who followed through as if he were starting a lawnmower. He released the ball with incredible finger rotation and whipped his arm skyward with a bent elbow. His production fell off during the early and mid-'90s, principally because of the erratic hooking action of reactive equipment. Having coached Monacelli in his early years on tour, I suggested a softer follow-through with greater extension and minimum elbow bend. The results were astounding as he assumed greater control. He had a better "read" on the ball and succeeded in harnessing all his power to a greater advantage.

For many years, Tim Criss was a journeyman on the PBA tour. Criss, pictured in the above photo, was one of the hardest-working players on the tour, but despite his diligent practicing night after night, he was rarely a threat and, more often than not, he ended up as a spectator. In the late '90s, he heeded my advice, abandoned his "behind the ear" follow-through in favor of a longer extension, and became an overnight success.

Perfecting the Follow-Through

Mistakes	Modifications
1. Ball is lofted upward on the lane.	**1.** Deliver the ball *into* the lane.
2. Elbow is bent and arm is recoiled in a violent manner.	**2.** Keep arm extended with minimum elbow bend. Do this by driving the fingers to the break point—no higher, no lower. The weight of the ball and the flow of the swing will produce a slight bend of the elbow on the follow-through. It must be natural, not forced or exaggerated.
3. Follow-through goes skyward with the fingers left of the face (for right-handers).	**3.** Follow through 90 degrees to the target.

As stated previously, a bumper crop of outstanding amateurs joined the PBA in 1998: Chris Barnes, Patrick Healey Jr., Kurt Pilon, Rudy Kasimakis, and Robert Smith. Not too surprising is that all possessed ideal follow-throughs. Barnes, a former Wichita State star and team USA member, has been the most successful of the '98 class. He recorded two titles in his sophomore season and is a threat in every tournament he enters. Barnes uses a fluid follow-through that delivers power through the fingers instead of the forearm. Rudy Kasimakis and Robert Smith possess two of the most powerful strike balls on tour. They perform with minimum effort, releasing low and long with minimum elbow bend.

In the event that some bowling scholars, coaches, or instructors disagree with my theories on proper follow-through, I don't want my methods of execution misconstrued as flimsy, fragile, or weak. Soft, in my interpretation, means a follow-through void of excessive force: silky and delicate, yet firm and fluid.

To sum up my suggestion for executing the ideal follow-through, keep the armswing low and long. Send the fingers to the break point—no higher, no lower. The weight of the ball may carry the arm and fingers slightly above this point; just don't exert any effort to *send* it up. A slight natural motion upward will not obstruct the ideal follow-through. Using no undue force in the delivery can also prevent early roll and preserve energy in the ball until it reaches the desired break point.

Remember . . . low, long, and fluid. Just let it flow!

7

Putting the Steps Together

Proper bowling execution incorporates several separate exercises. Although they are separate, they must be blended into a smooth, rhythmic manner. These are the principles involved:

☒ Stance (body position)

☒ Pushaway

☒ Free armswing

☒ Footwork (approach)

☒ Knee bend

☒ Hand position and release

☒ Follow-through

The following instructions are presented for right-handed bowlers; use the opposite if you're a left-handed bowler.

1. Assume a relaxed stance.

The stance, or the body position at the start of the approach, must be free of tension. Comfort rules! There are no set standards. Many bowlers

Brian Voss illustrates excellent technique, from stance to follow-through.

feel comfortable in erect positions, whereas others feel content in a semicrouched position. Either of these positions is acceptable as long as you are relaxed and comfortable. The main objective is to assume a position that enables you to begin your approach to the foul line with no restrictions.

Coaches and instructors have different views regarding the stance. I prefer the erect position because I'm a firm believer in a free armswing delivered from the shoulder joint. An erect position permits a freer flow of the arm than a lower or crouched position can produce. Many of the top PBA stars begin their stances from an erect position. Most notable in this respect are Mike Aulby, Chris Barnes, David Ozio, Brian Voss, and Walter Ray Williams. It is important to note that all these players exercise a long, free armswing initiated from a smooth pushaway.

However, witness the great successes of Norm Duke, Danny Wiseman, Marshall Holman, Steve Hoskins, and Rick Steelsmith, who start their approaches from a crouch. It may or may not be coincidental, but all of these players are small in stature. With the exception of Rick Steelsmith, all of them employ a semicontrolled armswing, yet they have one thing in common: their innate ability to relax the arm in the downswing.

2. Don't force the pushaway.

The pushaway is one of the most vital maneuvers in proper bowling execution. The pushaway, like the stance, can have optional features. Players who operate from a low crouch generally apply a semicontrolled swing. The majority of bowlers in this category use a lower outward pushaway and partially control the ball into the backswing.

Fundamentally, an ideal pushaway is one in which the ball is pushed slightly upward to create gravitational force. This type of pushaway must not be exaggerated or too forceful. Although the grip in the ball is firm, the pushaway is soft and delicate, just sufficiently arced to permit the ball to free-fall into the backswing.

Brian Voss possesses the greatest fundamentals in bowling. He epitomizes a model pushaway: extended, delicate, unforced, and repetitious. He initiates his game with this classic pushaway, a maneuver that places him among the smoothest players in the game.

Mike Aulby's incredible success can also be attributed to his superb pushaway. However, on occasion, Mike tends to tilt in the pushaway.

The key to eliminating this flaw is to maintain the shoulders in the upright position. Do not follow the pushaway with the shoulders. This is a common error among many bowlers. This is one of the few flaws in Aulby's game that I have focused on during the 20-some years that I have coached him. Nevertheless, it hasn't prevented him from winning close to 30 titles, including all five major events: the PBA National (twice), the Touring Players Championship, the BPAA U.S. Open, the Tournament of Champions, and the ABC Masters (three times). No other player in the history of the game has won all five majors.

3. Adopt a straight, free armswing.

Armswing is the manner in which the arm travels from the pushaway to the release point. Leading instructors and coaches have varied opinions on proper armswing. Many players, particularly power players, push the ball away to the left, walk to the left, open up their shoulders to the target, and then unleash wide-arcing hooks. This is the pattern for modern players who delight in opening up the lanes by swinging from a deep inside angle to the outer part of the lanes. It is effective when lanes are dry on the outside. This permits the ball to enter at a wide angle and create a greater strike percentage. With modern equipment, though, it can result in some of the weirdest splits imaginable.

Many notable coaches recommend the figure-8 swing or a modified figure-8. In a true figure-8 swing, the ball is swung into the pushaway with the hand under the ball. As the ball is approximately three quarters of the way into the backswing, the thumb of the hand turns down and in to the left, then reverses its movement back to the right and under the ball, actually forming a figure-8 as it begins its descent into the forward swing. Years ago, the figure-8 was a common maneuver among star players. The modern method (for right-handed players, opposite for left-handers) starts the pushaway toward the left of the body, forcing the swing to bump out to the right away from the body. As the arm reaches the top of the swing, the arm and hand form a half figure-8, then veer back toward the body line, descending in a straight path. The objective is to keep the hand under and inside the ball.

During the early '40s, Ned Day was one of the original figure-8 bowlers. The Milwaukee star was one of the most artistic bowlers of his era—smooth as silk, perfectly balanced, and seemingly flawless. Day was the classic figure-8 bowler. Don Johnson, one of the most dominant PBA players in the '70s, was a semi-figure-8 player. Johnson's backswing was straight as an arrow. He began his figure-8 on the forward swing and applied it solely through the hand down to the release point. His follow-through, however, took a different course, a point we will address later. Wayne Zahn, another star of the '60s and '70s, used the same type swing as Johnson's with one particular exception: his follow-through, which we will also review later.

The figure-8 swing is a matter of preference. However, this manner of execution presents a possible stumbling block. The figure-8 swing involves excessive movement in the backswing. This, in turn, necessitates realignment. I firmly recommend the straight armswing simply because the straight armswing eliminates inordinate movements that necessitate adjustment.

If armswings following an inside-outside course are not properly adjusted, one of two mistakes can occur:

1. The ball will squirt to the right.

2. Improper realignment will result in a pulled shot to the left.

An outside-inside swing will also necessitate realignment; otherwise it will follow a natural course to the Brooklyn side of the pocket (for right-handed bowlers, opposite for left-handers).

With all due respect to bowlers, amateur or professional, whose armswings necessitate realignment, I strongly recommend an armswing that follows a straight path from the pushaway into the backswing and continues through the forward swing, concluded with a *straight,* extended follow-through.

4. Carry out a balanced, rhythmic approach.

Footwork describes the pattern of your steps in the approach. Pacing the approach is one of the most important elements in proper execution. It is the basic foundation for rhythm and timing, two ingredients that are so vital for pinpointing release. Improper tempo will result in either early or irregular late swings.

Unfortunately, in various areas of coaching and instruction, many students and advanced bowlers aren't receiving the proper information. For example, many bowlers who do not drift in their approach (those who walk in a straight line) are instructed to slide on the same board on which they began their approach. This is a serious error in judgment.

The sliding step *must* finish directly in line with the preceding step, the power step. The power step is the third step in a four-step approach or the fourth step in a five-step approach. When you slide in line with the power step, your hips will be cleared for the descent of the forward swing. This will also keep your swing close to your body and prevent the flying elbow. It will also aid in eliminating a pulled shot. Equally as important, this maneuver forms a tripod for balancing the body. If your sliding foot does not move in under the previous step, the right side of your body, coupled with the weight of the ball, will create an imbalance, causing you to fall to the right. In doing so, you misdirect the ball. This strategy isn't confined to those who walk in a straight path. Bowlers who drift to the right or left must adhere to the same system: Slide in line with the previous step.

The ideal cadence in foot patterns permits the slide to arrive at the foul line a fraction of a second before the release point. This will allow you to be firmly planted, wait for the swing to descend to its flat plane, then release the ball at its greatest leverage position.

5. Bend the knee for a low release.

The knee bend is one of the requisites in proper bowling execution. It was the most positive force for Don Carter, recently acknowledged by the Bowling Writers Association of America as one of the three greatest players of all time. Carter used a crouched position and shuffled to the foul line with his nose seemingly to the ground. He kept his elbow bent throughout the swing and practically pushed the ball down the lane. In fact, Carter did his approach in a manner totally opposed to fundamentals, except for one important factor: his knee bend, which made him one of the most accurate shotmakers in the game.

Although a deep knee bend is the most important element in releasing the ball into the lane from a low position, several PBA bowlers have done very well without deep knee bends. David Ferraro and Ryan Shafer are two such examples. Dave Ferraro, now retired from the tour, won nine titles, despite the fact that he retired in his prime. Ryan Shafer came into his own in 2000-01, won three titles, and became one of the top five performers in the game. Although Ferraro and Shafer have almost no knee bend, both release the ball in a downward trajectory—that is, into the lane rather than upward on the lane. Therefore, the deep knee bend, which provides a low release of the ball into the lanes, will generally provide the best result.

There are conflicting opinions among some bowling instructors regarding proper knee bend. Although there is justifiable emphasis placed on bending the sliding step, we must underscore the step preceding the slide—the *power step*. (The following information assumes a four-step approach for right-handed bowlers, the opposite for left-handers).

The power step is the most meaningful step of the entire exercise. It is the catalyst for descending into a slide. This enables a bowler to release the ball from a low angle. The power step is used to push off into the slide in a low, firm position. This also prevents the body from rearing up at the line.

A deep knee bend in the third step of a four-step delivery can be more effective if it is short and rapid. This permits a bowler to descend more easily into a sitting position. A long third step will hinder any attempt to "take a seat," creating a block in the knee bend and resulting in the bowler's rearing up after the initial slide.

A deep knee bend is the trademark of such current outstanding PBA stars as Jason Couch, Brian Voss, and Norm Duke. It was also the strong suit for past bowling greats Don Johnson, Dick Ritger, Jim Stefanich, and Ray Bluth. Marshall Holman, recently honored by *ABC Magazine* as one of the top 20 greatest bowlers of the century, attained his lofty standing by virtue of a deep knee bend that concluded in a low, outward path.

Mike Aulby, despite his incredible record, does have one chink in his armor. Though his record seems to refute the importance of a good knee bend, Aulby is prone to occasional slumps, because of his sporadic failure to descend on his power step. In coaching Aulby during the past 20 years, I have focused on this area of his game. Aulby isn't alone among successful players on the PBA tour who do not possess textbook knee bends. Justin Hromek, Bob Learn, Butch Soper, Dave Traber, and Jess Stayrook all have fared well in the pro ranks despite their inability to execute ideal knee bends. With the exception of Jess Stayrook, all are rather short in stature, an advantage that permits them to release a ball from a low position.

Again, I relate the exceptions, yet I always want to state the rule: A deep knee bend is one of the requisites for proper execution.

6. Wait for the proper release point.

A strong release is the envy of all bowlers. Many great players are blessed with this talent; others develop a desired release through study and practice; others are simply unable to master this important manner of execution. Nonetheless, many bowlers achieve great success by relying on accuracy and simplicity. A strong release is the ability to place the ball well back in the hand and the patience to wait for the proper release point to maintain the hand position until the last moment before removing the thumb. The next element is to drive the ball off the front part of the hand into the lane with strong finger rotation.

A strong release requires exact timing.

During the rubber and polyester bowling ball era, it wasn't uncommon to see good players release the ball on the upswing. This was a technique referred to as *lift and turn*. This method of execution was not as critical a flaw as it is today because balls made in the past did not have the gripping characteristics of today's modern missiles.

For those who are not naturally inclined, it can become quite difficult to coordinate the release at the proper release point. This is a practice involving movements that demand split-second synchronization. They go together or go nowhere. A great release at the improper release point is counterproductive.

The ideal release point is an area at or a little behind the ankle in the downswing. Take the thumb out, transfer the weight of the ball to the fingers, and drive the ball from the strongest leverage point. The release point should be approximately six or seven boards from the sliding foot, provided the slide is in line with the previous step.

During the '70s and '80s, Marshall Holman had the consummate release. It set a model for many contemporary bowlers. Holman was once featured on a Brunswick promotional slow-motion cybervision tape demonstrating his technique. Holman's release was lightning quick, but more impressive, the "Medford Meteor" had the knack to seemingly lay the ball into the lane. Holman's release featured a cupped wrist that collapsed at the release, then whipped forward through his fingers and into the lane. Several years ago, I was the technical adviser for Marshall Holman on an instructional video titled *Maximum Bowling,* which focused on fundamentals. Holman demonstrated the advantage of carrying out a superb release that corresponds with an ideal release point. The video also exposed the harmful effects of an early swing, particularly the damaging results of hitting up on the release.

Hitting up on the ball must not be confused with hitting *out* on the ball. Hitting up and lofting occur when balls are released in an upward motion and enter the lane in a bouncing fashion. Conversely, hitting out is feeding the ball into the lane, a manner of execution that has enhanced the careers of such stars as Walter Ray Williams, Pete Weber, Norm Duke, Brian Voss, and David Ozio.

Pete Weber, a great pure talent, has one of the cleanest releases ever. It appears effortless, yet it is among the most explosive strike balls in the sport. And, as Holman does, Weber lays the ball into the lane smoothly with no sound or bounce whatsoever. Holman and Weber confirm that excessive force and raw power are not necessary for a strong release; rather, exact timing in delicate fashion is essential. Holman and

Weber can best be described as power strokers, and although they exemplify the power stroke, they aren't alone in using this type of game.

There are two other categories of releases: pure strokers and crankers with raw power. The pure strokers include Mike Aulby, Parker Bohn III, Brian Voss, Dave Husted, and David Ozio, who rely on finesse and pinpoint accuracy.

Crankers exemplify raw power. They do not rely on finesse. They apply extreme wrist and finger rotation to create excessive revolutions. They are less exacting than strokers are and use their talents to create a wider pocket; that is, they deliver the ball to a specific area rather than a certain board. Power players are far more effective when the lanes afford wider angles to the pocket—angles that present a tremendous advantage in strike percentage. Power crankers are practically unbeatable when conditions favor their game. The most notable crankers on the PBA tour are Jason Couch (who is great on all conditions), Steve Hoskins, Brian Himmler, Rudy Kasimakis, and Robert Smith.

7. Extend your follow-through outward, not upward.

Equally important is the motion of the arm after the release, the all-important follow-through. The follow-through is one of the most significant mechanical elements in sports: You see it in baseball, football, basketball, billiards, track and field, tennis, golf . . . you name it. It's the culmination of most exercises that require the arms and legs.

Improper follow-throughs have been an Achilles' heel for baseball pitchers since the game began. They develop sore arms, are beset by control problems, hang curveballs, lose speed and movement on their fastballs, and slide into funks when they exercise their follow-throughs improperly. Basketball players who excel at long-range shooting rely on delicate follow-throughs to achieve their goals. Golfers who drive balls in the 300-yard range would be ordinary mortals but for crisp and undeterred follow-throughs. Improper follow-throughs on putting greens have been the bane of many pro golfers.

In bowling, inferior follow-throughs have hampered many players. This is partially due to the various methods being taught in today's game. As a practicing coach and instructor, I find it disconcerting to be critical of other teachers. However, because of the modern trends in bowling equipment and lane maintenance, the physical aspect of the game has evolved.

The fundamentals are still the cornerstones for proper execution. Nevertheless, one of the most flagrant errors occurring in today's game is in the follow-through. This common flaw is an unfortunate carryover from the days of old rubber balls and shellac and lacquer finishes. These conditions demanded aggressiveness in the release and follow-through. Players were taught to lift and turn the ball and to reach for the ceiling on their follow-throughs. The game now features bowling balls made of materials that generate greater friction on the lanes. Manufacturers no longer are confined to making old pancake blocks that merely serve to counterbalance the weight removed in drilling. Research and development geniuses spend hundreds of thousands of dollars on developing sophisticated weight blocks that are placed in strategic areas of the ball for additional power. Also, educated drillers are now able to place weight blocks in such a manner that they can virtually control hook patterns in any ball, on any condition, and at any desired break point.

In this era of active, reactive, and Proactive equipment, overly aggressive follow-throughs that head skyward are actually detrimental to a bowler. Modern balls require the bowler to use more finesse. A moderately stroked ball is far more effective than one that is delivered too aggressively. This is due to the gripping characteristics in modern missiles that result in overreaction. Balls with excessive revolutions tend to hook too sharply. Those delivered in a more delicate manner move in a gradual arc.

Power bowlers Harry Smith, Bill Lillard, Carmen Salvino, Buddy Bomar, and Dick Hoover applied the old style of follow-through (lift and turn and reach for the ceiling) and were extremely successful. Nonetheless, many great bowlers defied this logic and directed their follow-throughs out toward the pins. Bowlers such as Don Carter, Billy Welu, Tom Hennessey, Joe Joseph, and Junie McMahon all ended their deliveries toward the pins.

Thunderous upward follow-throughs spin while airborne. The ball reacts immediately on contact with the lane. Conversely, a ball delivered low and out toward the pins is more inclined to have the textbook action bowlers seek: skid, roll, and hook.

One of the best components to a proper follow-through is the softening extension of the fingers and arm. The fingers extend outward, *not* upward, to the break point. Make a concentrated effort to keep the arm extended with little or no bend in the elbow. You can only accomplish this if you deliver the swing from the shoulder. Any delivery that is generated from the forearm negates any possibility of a proper follow-through.

A couple of quotes from two astute students of the game support my position on proper follow-through. Earl Anthony subscribes to this theory: Follow the ball with your hand. Tom Kouros, one of the greatest coaches in the game, recalls some sage advice from Junie McMahon, an all-time great: Direct your follow-through to the pins. They are down there. McMahon, pointing to the pin deck, told Kouros, "When they place them up in the ceiling, you can direct your follow-through up there."

Armed with these words of wisdom from such bowling luminaries regarding this phase of the game, I highly recommend a softer, longer extended follow-through as part of the ideal execution and one of the seven steps to success in bowling.

A quality follow-through can enhance your game in several manners. It plays an integral role in maintaining proper balance and it is chiefly advantageous in mastering ball reaction. Excessive vigor in the follow-through, particularly inordinate force generated from the elbow, will greatly affect the hooking pattern of the ball on its path to the pocket.

Gauging the Right Amount of Hook

How much hook does a bowler need to be successful? Any hook with sufficient drive into the 5-pin is satisfactory. Utilizing proper angle and speed, an effective hook carries the 5-pin, which is the prime objective of a strike shot. (Grips, spans, and pitches play a major role in gauging hooking patterns. This is addressed in chapter 12.)

Hook is the means, but it is not the end. Big hooks are in no way the prerequisite for successful scoring. For example, Hank Marino, voted the top bowler in the first 50 years of the game by the Bowling Writers Association of America, threw a small hook with deadly accuracy. The diminutive Italian used a tight thumbhole in a two-finger grip. He often placed his thumb in the finger hole when the thumbhole loosened a bit. Marino was in the minority for choosing a tight-fitting thumb. The majority of top professionals prefer thumbholes that are snug enough to prevent squeezing or dropping the ball yet afford quick releases.

Joe Wilman, a great bowler from the Midwest, won the 1951 All-Star Championship, finished second twice in this prestigious tournament, placed second in the 1951 Masters, and bowled his way into the ABC Hall of Fame with one of the shortest hooks in the game. Dick Hoover, the most accurate bowler in history, threw a slight hook, straight and hard. Hoover's record includes the 1951 All-Star Championship and back-to-back ABC Masters titles in 1956 and 1957. Although Hoover's excessive speed resulted in numerous 5-10 splits, he was no worse than an even bet to convert these splits into spares. ABC Hall of Famers Joe Norris and Joe Joseph, two of the smoothest and silkiest strokers of their era, delivered slight hooks with little effort and deadly accuracy.

Marion Ladewig, the unanimous choice among bowling experts as the greatest female bowler of all time, dominated the game as no one else, male or female. She was selected Bowler of the Year nine times, more than any woman in the history of the game. As her male counterparts did, she delivered a straight ball, was exceptionally accurate, and rarely missed the pocket.

Understanding the Path to the Pocket

In determining the amount of hook required, one must understand the workings of a ball in its path to the pocket. When a ball is released, it will enter three phases of activity in its path to the target. See figure 8.1.

☒ **First phase**—The first stage a ball enters is the skid phase. Normally a ball will skid from the moment it makes contact with the lanes through the first third of the lane (roughly 20 to 30 feet, depending on the amount of oil applied to the heads). The heads are the first 15 feet of the lane and are made of hard maple that can withstand the continual pounding of the ball.

☒ **Second phase**—During the second phase of the ball's course, it makes contact with the next 45 feet of the lane, which is constructed of pine. Pine is softer than maple. The ball makes greater contact with the lane, and the motion of the ball continues toward its target sideways. This, in bowling jargon, is termed *side roll*. The ball continues on its course to roughly three to five feet from the pocket. At this point, the ball reaches its maximum forward trajectory, or *full roll*, and makes its leftward move into the pocket.

☒ **Third phase**—For the third phase, let's examine the ball's reaction on entering the pocket. On a right-hander's ideal strike shot,

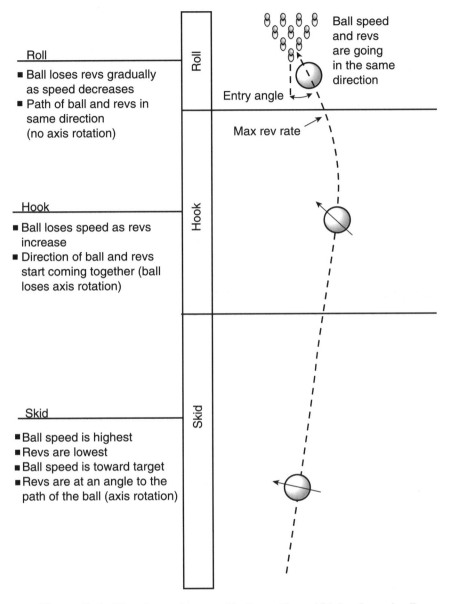

Figure 8.1 The three phases of ball reaction: skid, hook, and roll.
Reprinted, with permission, from MoRich Enterprises, Inc.

the ball will come in contact with only four pins, the 1-3-5-and 9. All others are erased by domino effect, better described in bowling terms as *pin deflection* or *pin action*. The 1-pin takes out the 2-pin, the 2 deflects into the 4, which deflects into the 7-pin; the 3-pin takes out the 6 and sends the 6 into the 10; and the 5-pin takes out the 8. This is generally regarded as the ideal strike shot.

However, strikes have been recorded in a variety of other ways. For example, balls entering the pocket late (that is, slightly behind the head pin) can result in strikes when the 6-pin is brushed by the 3-pin, which slides into the kickplates (sideboards), then bounces back into the 10-pin. More often than not, the 6-pin will lie lazily in the channel and result in what is termed a *weak 10*. On other occasions, misguided shots have crossed over to the Brooklyn side (left-hander's pocket, the 1-2 pocket). These strikes can be credited to lady luck. Additionally, a series of strikes can emerge from light hits that scatter pins into the left kickplates then ricochet back into assorted pins still standing: the 5-pin, the 2-4-5 pins, or any other single or combination of pins that have remained on the deck. These fortunate strikes are referred to as *wall shots* and are also categorized as lucky.

Examining Different Ball Tracks

Before proceeding further, let's examine ball tracks, the ring formed around the ball resulting from the ball's contact with the lane and its subsequent entry into the pocket. (See figure 8.2.) There are seven types

Straight ball

Back-up ball

Full roller

Semiroller

Full spinner

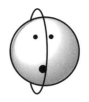

End-over-end roll

Figure 8.2 Different ball tracks.

of ball tracks that indicate the spin applied to the ball and the impact it will have on the pins:

1. Straight ball

2. Back-up ball

3. Reverse hook

4. Full roller

5. Semiroller (or semispinner)

6. Spinner

7. End-over-end roll

In chapter 5, we reviewed five ball paths to the pocket. Although seven different variations of ball tracks may appear on a ball, tracks are the result of different releases that produce disparate results.

Straight Ball

Throughout the history of the game, bowlers have been taught and conditioned to hook the ball, and understandably so. A ball hooking into the pins produces a far greater percentage of strikes. This is by no means meant to demean a delivery that is directed in a straight line from a wider laydown point at the foul line. Those who doubt the effectiveness of a straighter shot need only consider the success of some straight shooters who have bowled their way into the ABC, WIBC, PBA, and PWBA Halls of Fame. The game is sprinkled with great bowlers who more than held their own by using straighter shots; relying on speed, angle, and precise timing; and covering less area in their path to the pocket.

The straight ball is released from an open hand with no rotation of the fingers whatsoever. The straight shot rolls over the center of the ball, often over the fingerholes or thumbhole. The track on the ball creates a noticeable rumbling sound when proficient players like Walter Ray Williams and Norm Duke, two of the deadliest spare shooters in the game, throw at single pins.

During the late '40s, '50s, and early '60s, Marty Cassio, a Rahway, New Jersey, sharpshooter, stood at the right side of the approach, fired directly to the pocket (and subsequently into the ABC Hall of Fame) using a straight shot. Tony Sparando, another Easterner and ABC Hall of Fame member, used a straight shot and more than held his own with the best of his era. However, they were exceptions. The straight ball is basically ineffective as a strike shot. It has little or no power entering the pocket, and the deflection factor makes it a hazardous venture. Consequently, very few professional bowlers employ this type of delivery for strike shots. However, many elite players have the ingenuity to use it for single or two and three closely bunched pins that require no lateral movement of the ball. However, not to be overlooked, straight balls are not in the minority among senior citizens or beginning bowlers. This, of course, is due to the simplicity of releasing the ball with minimum exertion.

Back-Up Ball

The back-up ball is the least desirable of all shots. It has no redeeming factor as a strike shot because it rotates in a path away from the pocket. Although the track on this type of ball covers almost the entire circumference of the ball, the carrying percentage is substantially reduced. This is due to its deflective effect on contact with the pocket, particularly in its inability to carry the 5-pin. Despite its deficiency as a strike ball, it has its positive use in some players' arsenals. For example, Norm Duke at times will throw a back-up ball at 10-pins, depending on lane conditions. Mark Williams throws a back-up ball at the dreaded 2-8-10 and has on occasion converted this seemingly impossible split. But the back-up shot is hardly regarded as an offensive weapon.

Reverse Hook

A reverse hook is executed in the same manner as a back-up ball, with one major difference. Although both hand and finger motions rotate in a clockwise direction, the reverse hook is delivered with a stronger drive of the fingers from right to left, thus creating a pronounced hooking effect rather than the slower fading roll of the back-up ball. Except for Ernie Hoestery, no notable bowler ever notched a reputation delivering a reverse hook. Hoestery, a star player from the '40s to '60s, sported a 200-plus average during an era when only the top players in the nation recorded 200 averages. Hoestery, a right-hander, stood on the left side of the approach (left-hander's stance) and released a reverse hook into the 1-2 pocket. Hoestery's ball had the same hooking effect as that of any left-hander, and, unlike the average back-up ball, it drove through the pins with little or no deflection.

Full Roller

The full roller is exactly what its name implies. The track on the full roller is formed between the thumb and finger holes, thus signifying an entry to the pocket with half of the ball on each side in the pocket. During the '40s and early '50s, this type of roll was effective on shellac lane finishes. Many star bowlers delivered full rollers, including Ned Day, Dick Hoover, and Billy Golembiewski, all ABC Hall of Famers. During the late '30s through the early '40s, Ned Day was one of the most dominant players in the game. The highlight of his career was his victory over Paul Krumske for the 1944 All-Star Championship. Day, a true practitioner of the full roller, was unlike two other full-roller bowlers, Billy Golembiewski and Dick Hoover. Billy G was a down-and-in player whose ball entered the pocket from a slight angle. On the other hand, Hoover combined incredible speed and accuracy: an "atom" shot (right at 'em, that is) right to the pocket, hard and straight. Conversely, Day delivered a slow, wide-arcing ball that crossed many boards and entered the pocket with tremendous force.

Lacquer lane conditions replaced shellac and proved detrimental to bowlers who delivered full rollers. Although Billy G and Hoover continued to bowl well into the '60s, Day, seriously hampered by the new lane conditioners, disappeared from the bowling scene.

A full roller is thrown with the hand in a suitcase position at the starting point. *Suitcase,* in bowling vernacular, is precisely what the term indicates. The fingers and thumb are lodged in the ball in the same way as one would carry a suitcase: on top. The hand remains in this position until the point of release. The thumb, at this point, is approximately at 10 o'clock. As the thumb exits, the fingers hit back and out in a clockwise motion with an open hand. Although a full roller tracks across half of the ball, it lacks the power produced by a side turn and enters the pocket more weakly. When shellac lane finishes gave way to lacquer applications in the early '60s, this was the first indication that full rollers were losing their effectiveness. It prompted better bowlers to alter their games by applying greater side turn to the ball. Unfortunately, it diminished the careers of those who were unable to modify or adjust their releases. To my knowledge, no bowlers on the current PBA tour throw full rollers.

Semiroller

People in some regions refer to this delivery as the *semiroller;* people in other regions refer to it as the *semispinner.* (Also, in some areas of the country, oily lanes are regarded as *slow lanes,* whereas people in other regions describe slick conditions as *fast tracks*.) At any rate, the semiroller, or semispinner, track is the most preferred delivery among elite players. The tracks on these balls are outside the thumbhole and fingerholes and can vary in many ways. Some tracks are closer to the fingers and a little away from the thumb; others can be just the opposite.

The semiroller track is closely related to the full roller. Whereas the hand and fingers of the full roller are positioned on top of the ball before the release and rotate in a clockwise fashion, fingers in a semiroller are positioned at about 6 o'clock and rotate to 3 o'clock in a counterclockwise manner. Both tracks are very high and cover a greater circumference of the ball than the full roller. However, the semiroller track is just outside the fingers and thumb and is far more effective than a high roller because it combines the high-rolling effect with the side-turning movement to produce greater driving power into the pocket.

The semispinner is thrown with the hand well under the ball until the release point, at which time the thumb exits and all the weight of the ball is transferred to the fingers. At the release point, the fingers are positioned anywhere from 6 o'clock to 10 or 11 o'clock, rotate in a counterclockwise manner, then drive the ball into the lane in an outward direction. (See figure 8.3.)

At the risk of confusing bowlers who have been trained to lift and turn, the term *lift* is a misconception. Perhaps *propel* or *project* would better characterize the most suitable method for a proper release. *Lift* implies releasing the ball in an upward movement. Because the pins are on an even plane with the release area, it seems illogical to release in an upward course. The ball must be delivered *into* the lane, not up and onto the lane.

Proponents of the semiroller include smooth strokers like Parker Bohn III, Chris Barnes, Brian Voss, Pete Weber, and Dave Husted. Some semirollers are thrown with minimum finger turn, thereby applying less hook and maintaining greater control. This was the system used by Don Carter and Earl Anthony, two of the most accurate players in history. They were uncanny at repeating quality shots in crucial situations and avoiding difficult spares.

Paul Colwell, an eight-time PBA titlist and winner of the 1974 ABC Masters, employed a Frisbee release—that is, a release akin to tossing a Frisbee. The hand is in a suitcase position until the release point. Then a quick exit of the thumb, then rotation of the fingers in a clockwise manner, up, then out and away. Despite the fact that Colwell's release resembled that of a full roller, Paul's ball track was outside the thumb and fingers and was categorized as a semiroller. The list of great bowlers of the past who threw semirollers would stretch for miles.

Many older superstars delivered semispinners with excessive finger rotation. This group executed with less precision but, by virtue of creat-

Figure 8.3   Rick Steelsmith illustrates a semiroller.

ing a greater pocket, they compensated by producing explosive strike shots that did not require the exactness of the lesser-hooking balls. This was the forte of such older power players as Bill Lillard, Don Johnson, Carmen Salvino, Harry Smith, and Andy Varipapa.

Spinner

A spinner tracks on the bottom third of the ball. In this type of ball, the wrist makes a spinning motion and the fingers end up on top of the ball at the release point. Naturally, with this type of track, the ball makes far less contact with the lane than one with a higher track. Although this is

121

the least-favored roll among elite bowlers, it served well for old-time stars Joe Norris and Joe Joseph.

The spinner shot is the opposite of a full roller, end-over-end ball, or semiroller. It is far less effective on light hits and is ineffective on oily surfaces. Conversely, bowlers who throw this type of ball relish dry conditions and enjoy a greater advantage over players who throw wide hooks and labor to keep the ball in play. Bowlers on the PBA tour are often confronted with conditions that magnify hooking balls to such an extent that power bowlers (right-handed) are forced to deliver balls across the left channel to keep them in play. In fact, even the smoothest strokers are forced to move far to the left to lessen the hooking action on the ball and reduce the angle to the pocket. These conditions favor spinners and reduce others to mediocrity. Because this type of condition is not as prevalent on the PBA tour's well-dressed lanes, bowlers who rely on spinners are normally disadvantaged. This is substantiated by year-end records that favor hook-ball bowlers over spinners in every statistical category.

Several players on the PBA tour throw spinners. Tommy Baker has to be the leader of the pack (figure 8.4). Baker manages an explosive hook with one of the slowest deliveries on tour.

End-Over-End Roll

The end-over-end roll became especially effective with the advent of reactive urethane balls that maintain a direct path to the pocket with little or no deflection. This delivery has greatly enhanced the games of several players who have mastered it, particularly Walter Ray Williams and Norm Duke. Bowlers execute this delivery by applying maximum forward roll with the hand fully under the ball. The ball is thrust onto the lanes with virtually no side turn. The secret to this method of execution is minimum application of the ring-finger turn. A major key to this type of roll is accenting the release off the middle finger in an outward thrust. A quality end-over-end shot resembles a full roller in its rotational movement, with one exception: A full roller is tracked between the fingers and thumb and has no side roll whatsoever. An end-over-end roll is tracked just outside the thumb and fingers, and although the track covers almost half of the surface of the ball, it rotates slightly leftward. However, unlike a semiroller that evolves into a sharp hook, an end-over-end roll maintains an even arc and is far more controllable.

122

Figure 8.4 The spinner has served well for Tommy Baker.

Although semirollers enter the pocket with greater force and require less accuracy, end-over-end rolls enjoy some advantages:

☒ They are far more effective in carrying high 4-pins.

☒ They are less likely to leave the 9-pin.

☒ They rarely leave such unsightly splits as the 2-8-10, the 2-4-6-8-10, or other leaves resulting from sharp-hooking balls that snap suddenly on dry back ends.

Walter Ray Williams stands head and shoulders above all others that rely on end-over-end deliveries. And, strange at it may seem, very few PBA players exclusively deliver this type of ball. Conventional wisdom would inspire others to emulate the all-time money leader and holder of over 30 titles, but to date, none have attempted to follow in his footsteps.

Norm Duke, considered to be as good as Williams, comes the closest to delivering an end-over-end ball as Walter Ray does. However, Duke, regarded as the most versatile player on the PBA tour, uses an assortment of hand positions, speeds, and angles to achieve his purposes. Nevertheless, he has resorted to an end-over-end release with great success.

Chris Barnes, another versatile player, has established a reputation for his ability to conform to all lane conditions. Like Duke, Barnes can throw straight, hook it a mile, or deliver it in an end-over-end fashion, all with equal success.

Determining How Much to Hook

The hand position in the release plays the greatest role in creating the amount of hook one desires. This brings us back to the question, "How much hook does one need?" Although bowlers have been successful with all degrees of hooking action, there is one principle that must be adhered to: Strikes cannot be achieved unless the ball carries the 5-pin. Wall shots have become prevalent, but competitive bowlers cannot rely on luck when championships and money are on the line. The 5-pin is the kingpin, the immovable object that challenges the irresistible force—the ball. Regardless of how hard or how soft the ball drives into the 5-pin, any contact greatly increases the possibility of a strike.

A weak 10- or a weak 7-pin is a possibility on any given shot. However, single pins are hardly a challenge to accomplished bowlers; and although the dreaded 8-10 leave is possible, it has been virtually nonexistent during the reactive ball era. Strikes recorded by virtue of wall-shot 5-pin blowouts lack quality execution. Any strike accomplished without the ball carrying the 5-pin is a result of luck. A 5-pin stand can result in a 5-7 split, a 5-10 split, a 2-4-5, a 2-4-5-8, or a 2-4-5-7-8—all difficult conversions. Conversely, single pins are duck soup compared to these dreaded leaves. Simply put, an effective ball has proper angle and speed and enough power to carry the 5-pin, the prime objective of an ideal strike.

Wide Hooks Versus Short Hooks

"Let your fingers do the walking" is a familiar slogan to anyone who has dialed a phone. With a slight modification, this catch phrase would serve as sage advice to bowlers: "Let your fingers do the work." Players who hook the ball have a great advantage over those who are not quite adept at this art. And those who can deliver power-laden missiles by using specific finger positions to alter the trajectory of the ball have, on certain conditions, an even greater advantage.

There are various classifications of bowlers: power players, strokers, spinners, and end-over-end shooters. These categories generally relate to the degree of rotation a bowler applies to the ball. Fingers play the major role in determining the direction of the ball and the amount of rotation one generates. Power players deliver wide-hooking balls by combining tremendous thrust of the arm, wrist, fingers, and legs. Strokers, on the other hand, rely more on finesse and delicate touch.

Power Players

Power players deliver wide-hooking balls with substantial wrist, finger, and leg action. This type of bowler uses power through force. The art of hooking a ball begins with the starting position of the fingers and wrist. The middle and ring fingers can be placed anywhere from the 6 o'clock, 7 o'clock, or 10 o'clock position, with the wrist rotating counterclockwise for a right-hander. The position of the fingers will determine the amount of hook; any of these finger positions can be effective, provided the thumb exits at the proper release point (that is, before the point in the forward swing where the hand begins to move outward).

To determine the amount of hook to use, let's begin with the largest hook potential—one practiced by PBA power players, the "crankers." The wrist is slightly cocked, the thumb is as far outside as possible, and the fingers are anywhere from 8 to 11 o'clock. Positioning the fingers in this delivery can begin with the pushaway or open up at the top of the backswing. The hand position must remain open until the ball is a few inches from the release point, the point at which the thumb exits the ball. The thumb must never remain in the ball beyond the ankle.

All power bowlers play wide-sweeping hooks and actually widen the pocket, sacrificing pinpoint accuracy for power. However, as stated previously, a power bowler's delivery is categorized by one of two distinct manners of execution. Most contemporary players perform with extremely open hands, whereas others, particularly those of the old school, cup their hands.

Some power players, including Jason Couch, Steve Hoskins, Amleto Monacelli (figure 8.5a), Robert Smith, and Pete Weber, open up their hands at the top of the backswing and apply an inside-outside rotation of the fingers to generate powerful revolutions. On the other hand, Doug Kent, Bob Learn, Mark Williams, Del Ballard (figure 8.5b), and George Branham cup their wrists to deliver explosive missiles. Players who cup their hands generally possess less speed than do the open-hand players. This is not to say that bowlers with more hooking action are more successful than players who use shorter hooks with greater accuracy. In fact, the winning percentage for the accurate shorter-hook players far overshadows that of the power players, with two notable exceptions: Pete Weber and Amleto Monacelli. Weber has bowled with uncommon power and accuracy for more than 20 years, overcoming all barriers during an era that has moved from polyester to urethane to reactive urethane and then to Proactive urethane. Despite some struggles

Figure 8.5 *(a)* Some power players, like Amleto Monacelli, prefer an open hand position, *(b)* whereas others, including Del Ballard, cup their wrists at the top of the backswing.

with the high-tech equipment in the mid-'90s, he has demonstrated uncommon flexibility in mastering the modern game. Although Weber is categorized as a power player, he applies enormous torque on the ball with a smooth, undeterred, free-flowing armswing, which is the hallmark of a stroker. Weber embodies the true meaning of "putting fingers in the ball." All his power is generated through finger rotation, following a clean, crisp thumb release, free and easy. Weber is the epitome of the power stroker.

Monacelli, on the other hand, is the essence of the genuine power player. Like Weber, Monacelli possessed power and accuracy. With the advent of Reactive Resin balls, Monacelli, who delivered with a wicked snap of the wrist and an exaggerated follow-through, faced difficulty in attempting to harness his powerful delivery. Amleto experienced inconsistent overreaction and fell into a minor slump. Having previously coached the affable Venezuelan, I arranged a practice session with him. I recommended a lower and less violent follow-through with greater extension. He practiced my theory and, in a short time, developed the proper combination. After this change, Monacelli returned to contention on the PBA tour.

Dave D'Entremont may come the closest of any player to using the Pete Weber power stroke. Gigantic compared to Weber, D'Entremont generates as much power as anyone on tour, and he does it in a flowing manner. However, he isn't as consistent as Weber. Rudy Kasimakis, also known as "Rudy Revs," earned his nickname through his knack for applying incredible revolutions to the ball. Unlike most players, Kasimakis combines incredible torque with greater speed than the average bowler. He executes his delivery with minimum effort, despite the fact that it is generated from an extremely high backswing. Rudy, like Weber, exemplifies "putting fingers in the ball." Some power bowlers are proficient and comfortable with wide-hooking deliveries. However, as with Monacelli, many of them have attempted to temper their shots to maintain greater control.

In summary, power bowlers generate greater revolutions on the ball than do other types of players. They cover more boards on the lane, sacrifice accuracy, widen the angle to the pocket, and rely on the ball's explosive contact with the pins.

Strokers

The number of boards the ball covers does not dictate effectiveness. The smart bowler takes what the lanes dictate. A ball covering 4 or 5 boards is as effective as one covering 10 or 20 boards because the name

Helping Robert Smith
Attain Power *and* Accuracy

Courtesy of the PBA

Robert Smith possesses the strongest strike ball on the PBA tour. Smith not only throws a wide-arcing ball but delivers it with greater speed than anyone. Before Robert joined the PBA tour, I coached him at San Diego University. He had stardom written all over him. Robert's release was awesome but he negated its advantage with an extremely forceful follow-through that culminated behind his ear. I advised him to temper his follow-through by extending his arm outward and minimizing the bend in his elbow. He heeded my advice, became a bigger star, and established a reputation in amateur ranks that earned him a spot on Team USA for international competition.

After joining the PBA tour, Robert experienced difficulty in controlling his wide-arcing ball. Since I helped coach the youngster at San Diego State University, I suggested a modified Sarge Easter grip to negate the violence of his strike shot. The Sarge Easter grip, for those who are not familiar with this drilling procedure, involves a regular fingertip grip on the middle finger span and reduces the ring finger to a conventional span. I further recommended a forward pitch in the ring finger, thereby considerably lessening ring-finger rotation, which reduces excessive side turn. In this manner, the ball maintains its power yet stabilizes the violent snap as it enters the pocket. Although Smith is far from an end-over-end player, his adjusted grip tempered the side roll and permitted him to perform with greater control. Not too surprising, Smith's converted grip led him to two titles, including the 2000 U.S. Open championship.

of the game is *angle*. A shorter hook into the pocket is far more effective than one entering from a severe angle because balls entering the pocket late will hang corner pins and, in many cases, result in ugly 7-10 splits.

PBA statistics show that strokers display greater consistency over a period of time than do crankers. Players who combine power with less effort (that is, power strokers) are generally among the leaders in all scoring categories. However, power strokers are not in abundance. For example, PBA power strokers such as Parker Bohn III, Chris Barnes, Jeff Lizzi, Rick Steelsmith, and Danny Wiseman all combine power with delicate strokes and minimum effort, yet they cannot be categorized solely as strokers, crankers, or tweeners (in between crankers and strokers). Tweeners are pure strokers who do not possess overwhelming revolutions in their deliveries, yet they apply sufficient drive in their strike balls to keep pace with the elite players on the PBA tour.

A free armswing is the prime ingredient for strokers. It is the simplest and most relaxed method of execution. Nevertheless, a stroker is walking a thin line; that is, a stroker must maintain a firm wrist without sacrificing freedom of the arm. A stroker's hand position should be maintained throughout the delivery. The hand should be under the ball with the fingers somewhere between the 7 or 9 o'clock position and the thumb at around 2 o'clock. The fingers must rotate counterclockwise to about 3 o'clock with the thumb never finishing farther left than 12 o'clock on the follow-through. A thumb finishing past 12 o'clock will result in excessive spin and weaken the shot.

Because of the simplicity of their method of operation, strokers enjoy greater advantages over power players and other types of bowlers. Strokers employ less exertion. They are always balanced, which minimizes errant deliveries. By covering less area on the lanes, strokers reduce the possibility of leaving difficult spares and splits caused by balls entering the pocket at extreme angles. Although quality strokers do not generate as many revolutions on the ball as do power bowlers, they apply sufficient drive to the ball to produce strikes in a more accurate manner.

Brian Voss heads the list of ultimate strokers, but the list must also include Mike Aulby, Parker Bohn III, David Ozio, Dave Husted, and Norm Duke. All of these players boast smooth, graceful approaches, clean releases, easy strokes, and soft follow-throughs. And they are always balanced. These strokers are perpetual cashers, consistent finalists, and perennial winners. They achieve their goals through finesse.

Physical problems brought about by thousands of games on the PBA tour—aches and pains and sore thumbs—seldom beset them.

Power players enjoy one great advantage. When lane dressings are dry and oil patterns have been altered by excessive play, bowlers are compelled to extend the ball's path to the pocket. This forces bowlers to move farther left (for right-handers, right for left-handers) to deter early hooking action. Bowlers must attempt to drive the path of the ball away from the normal target and seek a later break point.

9

Opening Up the Lanes

Modern bowling balls have given a new dimension to the popular phrase "opening up the lanes." The phrase refers to the widening of the track, or area, the ball covers on its path to the pocket. However, bowlers who delight in opening up the lanes must remember another popular adage, "the shortest distance between two points is a straight line," and learn to beat conditions that are extremely dry, particularly in the heads or front part of the lane. This is a condition that presents a sensitive predicament for players who rely on wide-arcing deliveries. How you go about opening up the lanes depends on what type of bowler you are.

Categories of Bowlers

Let's identify the strokers, power strokers, power players, and straight players on the PBA tour as examples for opening up the lanes.

Strokers

Strokers are identified by their soft, flowing armswings and impeccable approaches. They achieve optimum power with minimum effort. They are picturesque and perfectly balanced, and they symbolize the textbook manner of execution. History suggests that strokers have a big advantage in the PBA. Witness the tremendous success and longevity of current players Mike Aulby, Norm Duke, Dave Husted, David Ozio, and Brian Voss.

The task of opening up the lanes may be more difficult for the average stroker. The average stroker employs a smooth, undeterred free armswing with a slight acceleration at the release point. That style may encourage a stroker to exert abnormal arm speed to drive the ball through the dry area rather than permit the ball to flow through the entire delivery. However, a flowing follow-through must not be mistaken for a weak delivery. In fact, top-rated strokers, particularly players on the PBA circuit, may not generate as much energy into the pins as power players can, but they can compensate and produce as great a strike percentage as power players by lessening the entry angle to the pocket.

Power Strokers

Power strokers closely resemble pure strokers, with two exceptions. First, power strokers, like power players, drift leftward (for right-handers, opposite for left-handers), open up their shoulders, then realign their bodies on their deliveries. Second, they apply greater revolutions to the ball. Although they exert more effort in their releases, they manage to maintain a flowing pattern in their follow-throughs. Power strokers combine a stroker's minimum effort with a cranker's wider angle to the pocket. This category includes Pete Weber, Dave D'Entremont, Rick Steelsmith, Johnny Petraglia, and Del Ballard. Tim Criss would fit in either category. He combines great finger rotation with what may be the slowest ball speed on tour.

Power Players

Power players epitomize the word *power*. They deliver explosive missiles generated from extraordinary finger and wrist rotation. They sacrifice accuracy and create a greater area, and they can be dominant on conditions that favor wide-arcing balls. Pure power players exert far more effort than power strokers do. Players who play the power game, including Steve Hoskins, Amleto Monacelli, Bob Learn, and Brian Himmler, rely on extreme wrist and finger movement for excessive revolutions. As a result, they are far more comfortable covering wider angles. Power players and some power strokers use the entire lane, but there is one major dissimilarity between them: Pure power players expend greater energy and apply excessive torque and speed to achieve their desired goals.

© Sleeping Dogs Communications

Power players, like Steve Hoskins, use extreme wrist and finger movement to unleash potent strike balls.

Straight Shooters

Walter Ray Williams is the premier straight shooter on the PBA tour. His end-over-end roll has propelled him to more than 30 titles and branded him as the most dominant player of the '90s. His method of attacking the pins in a straighter path is far superior to those of other straight players. This is because in its path to the pocket, Williams' ball maintains its drive through the pins without the deflection factor that normally plagues straight players.

Straight players seldom play inside the 17th board and rarely, if ever, attempt to deliver the ball against the grain. Williams has mastered the

133

end-over-end roll and, although he isn't as proficient in applying rotation to the ball when conditions dictate the tactic, he still manages to do well. Other PBA stars that rely on the accurate straighter shot have not fared as well. Ernie Schlegel, Curtis Odom, Butch Soper, Dave Traber, and Roger Bowker have managed to make a living playing a direct line to the pocket, but this group is hardly among the elite. Schlegel, in 33 years as a pro, has collected only six titles. The rest haven't fared any better. Soper, in 27 years as a pro, has only six titles. Bowker, a 22-year PBA veteran, owns five titles. In 17 years as a pro, Traber has recorded four championships. Although Odom has knocked on the door several times in his 19-year stint as a PBA member, he has yet to capture a national title. With the exception of Walter Ray Williams, straight shooters appear to be at a disadvantage to those who angle their shots into the pocket.

Methods for Opening the Lanes

With this in mind, what is the proper manner for opening up the lanes? Opening the lanes requires a laydown point (the board on which the ball is released by a right-handed bowler) anywhere from the 30th to the 40th board. The ball will cross a section of the lane somewhere between the fourth and sixth arrow and reach a break point at an area between the 5th and 10th board. This is referred to as *bellying the ball.*

There are various ways to achieve this maneuver, depending on the amount of oil dressing that prescribes numerical combinations designed to drive the ball into the pocket. These combinations are equated by a minus and plus system relating to the board of the slide foot at the point of delivery, the board at the arrows, and the break point that arcs or angles the ball into the pocket. For example, to increase the angle to the pocket, shift your feet left one board and move your target one board to the left (for a right-hander). If your desired break point is not satisfactory, increase the movements right or left until you achieve the right results. In bowling jargon, these adjustments are referred to as 1-1, 2-1, and 2-2 moves and serve to increase or decrease the angle of the ball.

Figure 9.1 illustrates the angles necessary for lane conditions that are dry and require wider angles to the pocket. Moving away from the target with a bigger hook overcomes dry lanes in which the ball tends to hook too early.

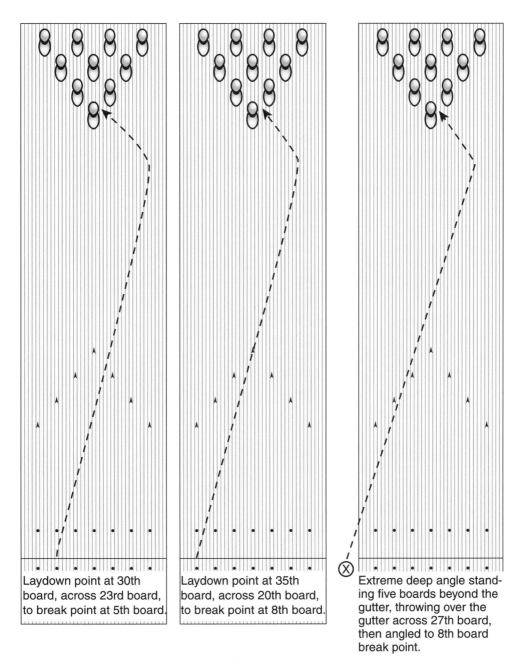

Laydown point at 30th board, across 23rd board, to break point at 5th board.

Laydown point at 35th board, across 20th board, to break point at 8th board.

Extreme deep angle standing five boards beyond the gutter, throwing over the gutter across 27th board, then angled to 8th board break point.

Figure 9.1 Moving away from the target and using a bigger hook helps overcome dry lane conditions.

Aligning Feet and Shoulders to the Target

The most conventional method of opening the lanes is to approach and address lanes with shoulders and feet squared to the target. For example, on conditions dictating a starting point on the left portion of the lane, an area beyond the 25th to the 40th board (for right-handers, opposite for left-handers), PBA standouts Brian Voss, Dave Husted, David Ozio, and Norm Duke address the lanes with their shoulders and feet toward the target. Although they tend to step slightly out of the ball path on the backswing, they maintain a square alignment with the desired target.

This is similar to a stance that most professionals use to shoot at the 10-pin, but there's one big difference. In addressing the 10-pin, there is no rotation of the fingers. In fact, the most proficient spare shooters flatten the shot to reduce or eliminate any hooking action, then project the ball in a direct line to the corner pin. Norm Duke actually delivers a straight ball, sometimes a back-up ball.

When strokers line up for a strike shot from a deep inside angle, in which the break point is between the 7th and the 10th board, they square their shoulders in that direction but, instead of flattening the shot for spares, pros will arc the ball to the break point and into the pocket with the fingers rotating counterclockwise.

On numerous occasions, strokers begin their approaches in front of ball returns, which obstruct any leftward movement in a bowler's initial stance (right-handed bowlers, the opposite for left-handers). Bowlers whose games depend on lining up with their target stand in front of the ball return and drastically shorten their steps. Through practice and perseverance, they have mastered the art of coordinating a free swing, a firm release, and sufficient speed for achieving their desired goals.

Shifting the Body and Realigning With the Target

Power players, particularly players who want to open up the lanes, subscribe to a different theory when ball returns prevent extreme starting positions. Some of today's players walk a straight line alongside the ball return, shift the feet and torso in front of the ball return, open their shoulders, then realign with the intended target. Conventional wisdom suggests this rapid shifting of feet, torso, and shoulders and realignment to a target is extremely difficult to perform on a consistent basis. Nevertheless, a select number of PBA players are carving out a nice living using this approach. Most of these players were weaned on contemporary bowling conditions and equipment. They emerged from the junior ranks and launched their careers during the urethane ball revolution. At the risk of sounding negative, I've got to say that any success achieved in walking to the left (figures 9.2, a and b), shifting the feet and torso, opening up the shoulders back to the right (figure 9.2c), and delivering a ball to a specific area (figure 9.2d) must be regarded as an exception rather than a rule. Contemporary players who perform in this manner have become proficient through hours, days, and years of practicing.

From an instructor's viewpoint, it's not a method of execution that warrants teaching. On the other hand, an instructor would be foolish to alter the style of anyone who has attained any degree of success. Right-handed players like Steve Hoskins, Bob Learn, Ryan Shafer, Brian Himmler and Pete Weber are among many PBA players that execute in this fashion.

Styles of the Pros

Pro players who use this approach—shifting and realigning to the target—have had varying degrees of success. Amleto Monacelli, an 18-time titlist, uses an open shoulder technique. He accentuates an open position by extending his nonbowling arm forward, then he drops his thumb with the palm of his hand facing the ceiling. This enables him to pull his right shoulder back, place his hand well under the ball, and further open his delivery. Monacelli achieved most of his victories on lanes that were conducive to wide-arcing shots, but he notched many of his wins on conditions that demanded greater accuracy. The Venezuelan sharpshooter has become one of the PBA's elite all-around players by virtue of his proficiency to alter hand positions and change speeds and his uncanny ability to read lanes.

Steve Hoskins has emerged as one of the most successful players who specialize in opening the lanes. The stocky Floridian has 10 titles to his credit. However, his formative years on tour were mediocre, at best. Although he was voted Rookie of the Year in 1989 by PBA players, he failed to cart a title in his first five years. In an earlier chapter, I mentioned setting up a practice session with Hoskins in 1993 wherein I made several suggestions I thought would improve his game. Fortunately, the recommendations I made proved to be effective. Two weeks later, he notched his first championship at Grand Prairie, Texas. Like Monacelli, Hoskins extends his nonbowling arm forward with his palms upward and unleashes one of the most potent strike balls in the game.

Bob Learn and Ryan Shafer also use the shifting and realigning approach. Learn holds more than 55 games of 300 in his career, and gained worldwide fame on national television in 1996 in Erie, Pennsylvania. He averaged 282 for the four-game TV show, which included a 300 game. But, aside from this record-shattering performance, Learn has had a sporadic career, recording only three other victories over an 18-year professional career.

Ryan Shafer joined the PBA tour in 1986 and was voted Rookie of the Year in 1987. Although he had failed to win in his early years on the tour, he managed to eke out a living while gaining valuable experience. Shafer had the record of earning the most money of any bowler without a title. He finally broke through with two victories in 2000 and has established himself as one of the top players on the PBA tour.

Brian Himmler, who joined the pro ranks in 1993 after an outstanding amateur career, is the epitome of the contemporary player. He approaches the foul line in an exaggerated drift to the left and opens his shoulders to the maximum degree. Himmler's five-step approach fea-

Figure 9.2 Although not recommended, some power players subscribe to the shifting and realigning approach. Here Brian Himmler (a) starts in a straight line, (b) drifts to the left, then (c) shifts back to the right to (d) deliver the ball.

tures a short, rapid fourth step that propels and powers him into one of the most destructive strike balls on the PBA tour. Although Himmler elevated his game to a higher level and established himself as a major force on the PBA tour during the past few years, he still has only one title.

In view of this limited success, it's safe to assume that the conventional approach of walking toward your target has a decided advantage over a leftward approach that requires a subsequent shift in direction, opening of the hips and shoulders, and subsequent realignment to the intended target.

With all due credit to Weber, Hoskins, Learn, Shafer, and Himmler, several other power players have not fared as well. Bob Spaulding, whose booming strike ball was among the most potent on tour, proved that power alone does not ensure success on the PBA tour. Spaulding's failure to moderate his devastating strike ball resulted in his retirement from the PBA tour. He struggled on drier conditions, and his erratic shots on anything less than a full rack branded him as one of the poorest spare

shooters on tour. Spaulding recorded his only title at Grand Prairie, Texas, in 1995, the same year Mike Aulby defeated him in the Brunswick Tournament of Champions. He won $109,927 in 1995 but his inability to temper his shot and his woeful spare game forced his retirement from the PBA tour.

Kelly Coffman, like Spaulding, was a prime example of wasted power. Regarded as possessing the most powerful ball on tour, Coffman delighted in applying maximum revolutions on the ball to warrant his reputation. Absorbed with his obsession to determine his potency and oblivious to the impending results, he seemingly derived greater satisfaction from ripping racks on light hits than from adjusting his game for solid pocket shots. Coffman, like Spaulding, was a perennial member of the Jowdy All-Miss Team. (The All-Miss Team is an annual column I write for publications that list five or six of the poorest spare shooters on the professional tour.)

Coffman's 12 years on the PBA tour were the greatest misuse of raw talent I have ever witnessed. He was strong, healthy, and extremely pleasant. His strike ball was second to none. To my knowledge, he never abused his body with drugs, tobacco, or alcohol. He had all the tools to be a winner. He could have and should have been a real star. I sincerely believed he had the makings of a winner on the professional circuit so, during a PBA tournament in California, I arranged a practice session and made several recommendations to diversify his game. Although the practice session provided instant improvement, he reverted to his normal method of execution in tournament play. Needless to say, he retired from the tour less than a year later with nary a title to his credit.

Throughout the country, youngsters are being weaned on soft conditions that favor wide-hooking balls. Thousands of 300 games and 800 series are recorded yearly, and players who specialize in opening up the lanes have rung up the majority of these honor scores. However, because of the overall practice of lane blocking to increase scores, these high marks have become insignificant. The true ability of a bowler is manifested on honest lane conditions. Such conditions are those offered by PBA maintenance crews and organized in sport leagues in bowling centers across the nation.

10

Mastering Shotmaking Strategy

Serious bowlers seek every advantage for striking percentage. They make concerted efforts to match equipment to the dictates of the lanes. Intelligent bowlers try to overcome conditions that are unresponsive to certain equipment by altering balls with different surfaces and assorted pin placements for weight distribution.

Unlike some other sports, bowling has standard, constant dimensions. A bowling lane is 42 inches wide and is constructed with 39 to 42 boards. It is 60 feet long from the foul line to the pin deck. The first 15 feet of the lane is constructed of maple, a surface that is capable of absorbing the brunt of 16-pound balls. The next 45 feet consist of pine.

Dots and arrows mark lanes. There is a set of dots six feet beyond the foul line. These dots precede a set of arrows beginning 15 feet beyond the foul line that dovetail toward the foul line. The arrows are placed five boards apart starting from either side of the gutter. The first arrow is on the 5th board, the second on the 10th board, the third on the 15th board, and the fourth on the 20th board.

The distance from the beginning of the approach to the foul line can vary, but it is usually about 15 feet. The approach is marked by three sets of dots, one about an inch behind the foul line, one 12 feet behind the foul line, another 15 feet behind the foul line. The latter two sets of dots are used for gauging a starting point. The various arrows and dots are implanted in the lanes to serve as targets and have become the main focus for precision execution by better bowlers.

These are the visible advantages that bowlers are afforded. However, bowling equipment geniuses have failed to create a device that clearly exposes oil patterns and oil carrydown—at least not to the naked eye. In addition to this, many bowling lanes are constructed (not necessarily by design) with a few boards that do not match others in texture or hardness. Any of these boards can seriously affect the roll of the ball and mar a quality-executed shot. With this in mind, a player must devise a method to avoid this particular area yet negotiate another path to the pocket.

Overcoming the Reverse Block

Most of today's bowlers perform on lanes that are dressed for high scores. On these lanes the oil is applied heavier in the middle and drier on the outside. This is the pattern of choice of a majority of bowling proprietors. Because these maintenance procedures supposedly are within ABC regulations, they have resulted in "legally" blocked conditions—conditions that have aided in shattering every scoring record conceivable. As of this writing, there have been no less than *five* 900 series recorded. Moreover, a complete league record average of 259 stood less than a full year before it was erased by an unbelievable 261!

Nonetheless, these conditions can become treacherous too. For example, lower-average bowlers normally throw the ball right down the middle of the lane. A continual flow of shots in the middle area of the lane will, in due time, push the oil to the outside part of the lane. The outside area then becomes slicker, the middle area dries out, and the result is a *reverse block*. The reverse block is the most difficult to overcome, particularly for hook-ball bowlers.

Straight-and-Hard Shot

I referred to a reverse block situation in chapter 2 when I described the strategy applied by Amleto Monacelli at the Showboat Invitational Tournament in 1988. Monacelli, a player whose forte is a wicked hook, overcame the reverse block by throwing straight and hard. (See figure 10.1.) He relied on high pin count to snatch victory. This is an example of ingenious shot strategy.

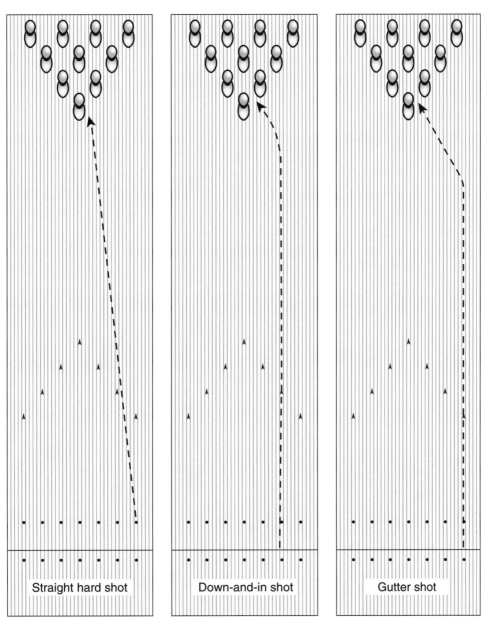

Figure 10.1 Strategies for overcoming the reverse block.

Well-dressed lanes that enable a player to repeat shots require no strategy, provided all fundamentals are exercised. However, quality shots on difficult conditions require strategic preparation. Monacelli's strategy was a brilliant maneuver. Nonetheless, on this type of condition, a bowler has two other options: the down-and-in shot and the gutter shot.

Down-and-In Shot

The down-and-in angle is a conservative choice. It is not to be confused with an outside shot delivered from an inside laydown point. To be more specific, in the down-and-in shot, the ball is pointed toward the pocket. (See figure 10.1.) It *cannot* be delivered in an arcing trajectory. Any attempt to arc a ball on a wet-dry condition is an invitation to disaster. If the ball begins its movement to the pocket at the break point

Figure 10.2 The gutter shot requires a delicate touch and precise timing. David Ozio *(a)* starts his approach on the extreme right side of the lane, *(b)* lays the ball down between the one and three boards, then watches as the ball *(c)* rolls along the edge and *(d)* hooks into the pocket.

a nanosecond too soon, overreaction rears its ugly head and, more often than not, a player is faced with unsightly splits: the 4-6, 4-6-10, 4-7-10, 7-10, 4-6-7-10, and perhaps the aforementioned splits with additional pins. On the other hand, if the ball is thrown with greater speed, it will hit the wet area and skid past the break point. In all probability, this type of shot will conclude in a variety of difficult leaves. For instance, the dreaded 2-8-10 split; a washout, which is a wide-open split with the head pin standing; or perhaps pin counts of five or less.

Gutter Shot

The third option is the *gutter shot*, shown in figures 10.1 (page 143) and 10.2. It can be a lethal weapon if executed with finesse and a delicate touch. A gutter shot is not arced, it isn't straight, and it is not pointed to

Photos courtesy of ABC Bowling Magazine

the pocket. It is delivered from the extreme right side of the lane for right-handers (opposite for left-handers) somewhere outside the first five boards in a straight trajectory to the break point. The ball is delivered with minimal side turn with an end-over-end release but not completely straight. Although this statement seems ambiguous, this is a recommendation reserved *only* for very skillful bowlers—specifically bowlers who have complete command of hand positions, speed, and unforced follow-throughs. These players include Norm Duke, Gary Dickinson, now-retired Nelson Burton Jr., Walter Ray Williams, and the most prolific exponent of the gutter shot, David Ozio. Ozio has carved a Hall of Fame career with this type of delivery, one that requires incredible touch, precise timing, and above all, tremendous intestinal fortitude.

One might ask, "What's so difficult about this shot?" First of all, the laydown point of the delivery is on an area between the one and three board at the foul line (figures 10.2, a and b on page 144). The path of the ball follows the one or three board for approximately 40 to 45 feet (figure 10.2c), begins a gradual roll to about 55 or 56 feet, then abruptly hooks into the pocket (figure 10.2d). Keep in mind that a great portion of the ball hangs off the gutter for 40 feet or more, rolling within an inch or two of the edge of the lane. Any semblance of an outward trajectory spells disaster. This is why I recommend this type of delivery *exclusively* for the most proficient bowlers.

Although this precarious path of the ball constitutes a true gutter shot, many power bowlers execute gutter shots from deeper inside angles when lanes become extremely dry (except on wet-dry conditions). Right-handed bowlers are forced to move farther left (opposite for left-handers) on the approach to avoid the dry areas that offer little or no resistance to a hooking ball. In fact, on numerous occasions power bowlers began their stance beyond the left gutters (right gutters for left-handers) and release shots *over and across* the gutters to break points around the eighth board, 45 to 50 feet down the lanes. These are angles reserved for power players. These shots require great skill and often border on disaster. The perils of executing this line were never more in evidence than Del Ballard's fateful gutter shot against Pete Weber on a Saturday afternoon on ABC TV. Ballard entered the 10th frame of the championship game needing only six pins to seal a victory. Rather than play it safe, Ballard stuck with his game plan—a gutter shot—and saw his championship hopes evaporate as the ball dropped into the channel.

There's a lesson to be learned here which has been embraced by practically every professional and high-ranking amateur bowler in the world: *When counts of seven or better are needed to ensure victory, throw straight, hard, and make sure you hit the head pin.*

Straight shots have also become valuable assets for high-level and professional players who release wide-hooking balls. They use straight shots for single-pin conversions, particularly on corner pins that require little or no hooking power. In addition to throwing straight at all single pins, experienced players also shoot directly at the 1-2, 1-3, 2-4, 2-5, 3-5, 5-8, 5-9, 6-10, 2-4-5, and 3-6-10. These are conventional routines for great spare shooters like Walter Ray Williams, Norm Duke, Mark Roth, and Amleto Monacelli.

Overcoming Hooking Heads

One of the most challenging conditions facing bowlers is *hooking heads*. Hooking heads characterize the first 15 feet of the lane that has dried out and offers no resistance to the rotation of the ball. Freshly maintained lanes are oiled anywhere from the foul line to 25, 35, and sometimes 45 feet down the lane. On a freshly maintained condition, an average hook ball is in its skid stage for the first 20 to 25 feet. As friction increases, the ball assumes a rotational movement. Simply described, hooking heads are dried-out lane conditions caused by the ball's oil absorption. It is an area on the lane before the beginning of the ball's rotational path to the pocket.

Straight players are hardly affected by dry heads, and understandably so. Straight players execute in two fashions. They either apply greater spin on the ball or throw harder than average players do. Consequently, they are immune to dry heads and normally enjoy a greater advantage on these conditions.

Conversely, dry heads demand exhausting efforts from players who rely on ball rotation. Elite players exercise several systems in their attempts to overcome this dilemma. Many attempt to spin the ball through the heads. Others loft the ball *over* the heads, whereas some throw harder. Others simply move farther left on the approach (farther right for left-handers). Sometimes these options work, sometimes not; therein lies the dilemma. How can anyone maintain confidence in any sport if the impending results are enigmatic? Success can only be achieved through consistency of quality execution. As I've said before, success breeds confidence.

I have reservations about the aforementioned practices. First of all, spinning the ball through the heads is risky because of the difficulty involved in controlling the break point. Second, a ball delivered with excessive speed can disrupt the rhythm process for a bowler whose game is contingent on smooth stroking execution. Third, I have long expressed opposition to lofting the ball up and out on the lanes. Any ball lofted upward spins in midair before making contact with the lanes. Upon making initial contact with the lanes, the ball tends to bounce, go off line, and react irrationally.

Drag Shot

Although some bowlers are fairly successful and feel comfortable with any of these given exercises, I recommend one strategy that will influence every bowler's objective of getting through the dry heads yet maintaining a smooth, rhythmic approach. I refer to this delivery as a *drag shot*—a description so appropriate that it speaks for itself. This delivery does not deviate from a bowler's normal delivery. It requires just one delicate maneuver. On the release, extend the hand lower and longer with the fingers as far as possible, with *no* upward lift (figure 10.3).

Figure 10.3 David Ozio demonstrates the drag shot.

Merely adhere to the description of the shot: *drag*. Drag the fingers, hand, and arm to the maximum extent in a smooth, flowing fashion. It's almost like pushing the ball down the lane. The rotating motion of the ball in its early stages is practically nil. It reacts as a knuckle ball and floats through the heads. During this process, the ball expends little or no energy and maintains all its power before entering the pocket. This was one of Earl Anthony's prime assets in his arsenal of strategic weapons that set him apart from other bowlers. Anthony's adroitness was evidenced in his ability to score exceptionally well—and capture titles—in tournaments that stifled all other left-handed players who seemed to be wallowing in the wilderness.

The Earl Anthonys of the bowling world are few and far between. Since the mid-'70s, Mr. Anthony has been the standard of bowling excellence. Although bowlers seeking to attain Anthony's stature in the game seem inconceivable, his modus operandi can serve as a great example for those who seek to approach his mark in the game. Anthony's mental game, combined with his innate ability to change hand positions, speed, and angles, placed him alongside Don Carter and Dick Weber as the three greatest bowlers in the history of the game.

Game Plan A and B

Versatility is the key for bowlers who seek to perform at the highest level. Tiger Woods is one of golf's greatest attractions and, perhaps, the most charismatic personality in the world of sports. After one of his many victories, Tiger issued the following statement: "I didn't have my 'A' game today." Numerous PGA players, plus anti-Tiger golf fans, misinterpreted the remark, thinking Woods was showing too much cockiness. But this does not fairly depict his character. Tiger Woods is a winner, a student of the game, and, as all real champions do, he strives for perfection. And, as all athletes that set their goals above others do, he can resort to alternatives to perform at a level of excellence—a "B" game and perhaps a "C" game, but he is always striving for the "A" game.

In baseball, pitchers have been known to subdue their opponents even on days when they aren't in total command of their best pitches. We often read that Greg Maddux, Roger Clemens, Tom Glavine, and other top-rated Major League hurlers, after adding another victory to their great records, say things like "I didn't have my best stuff today, so I just tried to rely on good location." This is when you know they have resorted to their "B" game, banking on control and pitching to batters' weaknesses.

Michael Jordan, generally acknowledged as the greatest basketball player in the game, averaged more than 30 points a game for his career. Yet, when he wasn't pouring in 35 to 50 points a game, he stifled opponents in many other ways: defending his man, blocking shots, stealing the ball, setting picks, making assists while being double- and triple-teamed, doing whatever it took to win . . . with his "B" game.

Superior athletes use their various skills to win. One-dimensional players seldom attain the height of success that consummate athletes do. The highest compliment in sports is when an athlete is described as being able to do it all. This applies as much to bowling as it does to any other sport. Versatility is the key to performing at the highest level.

Bowlers can best be compared to baseball pitchers, football passers, and basketball shooters. They are totally dependent on controlling a ball with the hand in an effort to hit a target. Pitchers can make an off pitch but get credited for a strike if the batter swings and misses. Football passers must master control of the ball, but they have the luxury of a Jerry Rice, Randy Moss, or some other acrobatic athlete who can turn a poorly thrown pass into a sensational reception.

Basketball players, like bowlers, must have total control of the ball. Both basketball and bowling have standard playing conditions. Other than basketball players having the advantages of home fans, all other conditions remain equal. There is, however, one glaring dissimilarity between basketball and big-time bowling. Although all bowling dimensions are identical, surfaces vary from lane to lane. The majority of league and recreational bowlers rarely face the difficulties that beset serious-minded amateurs and professional players.

In sharp contrast, the recreational bowler is catered to by proprietors who delight in posting high averages that can reach from 220 to 240 and up. Lanes are dressed and blocked in such a manner that anywhere from 20 to 40 pins can be added to a player's actual score. Honor scores like 300 games and 700 and 800 series have become commonplace during the past 20 years, primarily because ABC regulations covering lane conditions have been relaxed to foster a greater alliance between proprietors and the governing bodies.

But, conditions on the PBA tour and those laid down by various megabucks tournaments place a premium on quality shots that require both physical and mental ability. There are no blocked conditions. Lanes develop a greater diversity with assorted dressing patterns as oil is carried down, which wreaks havoc at normal breaking points. Any attempt to overcome these conditions with a single type of game will inevitably lead to an early exit from competition.

Game Plans of the Pros

Is it just a coincidence that players like Pete Weber, Brian Voss, Norm Duke, Chris Barnes, Parker Bohn III, and other top stars are consistently near the top in earnings and averages, regardless of lane conditions? Not at all! A close study of these superstars' games will reveal one basic principle: versatility. Each can immediately switch from an "A" game to a "B" game and sometimes to a "C" game. Each can throw coast-to-coast hooks that cover 20 boards. Each can play down and in. Each can play gutter shots and medium hook shots, go straight as an arrow, change speeds, or do whatever is necessary to be competitive.

"A" games vary from bowler to bowler, whether at amateur or professional levels. Walter Ray Williams Jr., the number one-ranked bowler on the circuit, deploys an end-over-end roll as his bread-and-butter weapon. His accuracy and ability to maintain sufficient speed for preventing rollout have given him the best carry percentage of any bowler on tour. The introduction of reactive bowling balls has proved to be a boon to his type of game. Before the advent of urethane balls, which generate added power, end-over-end rolls tended to deflect slightly, enough to leave weak 10s, 2-4-5s, or 2-4-5-8s. Perhaps more than any other player, Williams has benefited from reactive urethanes simply because of his precision in placing the ball in the 1-3 pocket.

Hard-driving reactive balls victimized Amleto Monacelli for several years. His "A" game featured a wicked snap of the wrist. He had great difficulty controlling the overreaction of his ball. Monacelli suffered the longest slump of his career until the latter part of the 1996 season. We arranged a practice session in which we worked on methods to calm the turn on his release when conditions dictated that he should. Monacelli has again become a force on the pro circuit, although he sometimes struggles when he waits too long to scale back the action on his release.

Dave Husted may be the most underrated player on the PBA tour—that is, except by his fellow pros. A 13-time PBA champion who has won three U.S. Open titles, the quiet, no-nonsense stroker goes about his craft without fanfare. Though he's recognized as one of the very best competitors on the tour, his businesslike performances have gone unnoticed by the press and the public, much as his adjustments in hand positions and speed have. After the introduction of reactive bowling balls, Husted's "A" game took on a completely different look. Even though he has decided to cut back his activities on the PBA tour, his steady performances continue.

Duke, Bohn, Voss, and Mark Williams all share one common trait: They are masters of hand positions and speed control. They can play all angles and change speeds, and all have adjusted their "A" games to comply with today's demanding conditions.

The versatility of Parker Bohn III helps him consistently place near the top in earnings and averages, regardless of lane conditions.

Your Own Game Plan

When you're experiencing problems in your game, the question then becomes when to switch from one plan to another and how that can be accomplished. First and foremost, you must understand that an "A" game is the one that has served you best and given you the most confidence, particularly at crucial periods when quality execution is imperative. Second, developing a "B" game with various hand positions and various speeds will pay big dividends. You *must* practice these methods on lanes that are not blocked and set up for easy scoring.

"A" Game: Forward Roll

When you are contemplating an "A" or "B" game, keep in mind that the friction created by today's modern bowling balls makes forward roll a premium. Is this too broad a statement? Let's examine the advantages of forward roll as opposed to the more explosive action of side roll.

Before the introduction of reactive urethanes, balls with terrific side roll resulted in powerful, thunderous strikes. This power was generated by tremendous wrist and finger application. That made for a great advantage to those who were able to master the art of making a sphere skid through the first third of the lane, slowly revolve into a roll for a short distance, and suddenly tilt into the 1-3 pocket, undeterred by the 10 pins it was intended to destroy. Such force, when properly administered, usually results in a strike.

Players who threw explosive hook balls included Pete Weber, Amleto Monacelli, Ron Palombi, Johnny Petraglia, and Marshall Holman. Review the records of these great players and you'll find they've been victimized by the creation of the powerful modern missiles, which require far less wrist and finger application. After several years of experimentation, Weber and Monacelli have made the proper adjustments. Johnny Petraglia shows occasional flashes of overcoming the urethane ball, but when Holman and Palombi encountered such difficulty in trying to decelerate their releases, they left the tour.

Bowlers whose "A" game is energized around an end-over-end roll are far more likely to be successful in today's environment. Consequently, their "B" game must evolve around less forward roll and additional side roll.

"B" Game: Side Roll

To apply more side roll, you must place the ball into the back part of the palm at the top of the backswing and keep it in this position throughout the forward swing. You can accomplish this by leading the downswing with the ring finger. This enables the hand to remain under the ball and keeps the elbow into the body, thus creating a straighter arm. This prevents "chicken-winging," or a "flying elbow." Several other methods have been suggested for preventing the elbow from flying out, such as directing the forearm to the target or closing the armpit. These prac-

© Sleeping Dogs Communications

Success in competition requires the ability to switch from an "A" game to a "B" game if the situation demands.

tices inadvertently create muscle tension in the forearm and tend to destroy a free, fluid armswing. A downswing led by the ring finger places all the weight of the ball at the bottom of the pendulum and enhances freedom of the arm.

To increase side roll, you must keep the hand under the ball to the point where it reaches a few inches behind the ankle. Here, the thumb exits and the fingers thrust forward. The ring finger rotates counterclockwise from roughly a 9 o'clock to a 3 o'clock position, approximately a half-turn of the hand. The thumb must never end up any farther left than the right side of your face on the follow-through, with the thumb pointed upward on the release. However, you must direct the release *outward*, not upward, and deliver (feed) it into the lane instead of up and onto the lane.

Forward roll should be far simpler to master. Instead of rotating the fingers at the point of release, you must concentrate the weight of the ball on the middle finger and release it from straight behind the ball in a forward motion—with *no* pressure whatsoever from the ring finger. The palm of the hand at the end of the follow-through should be facing the ceiling. You should maintain enough speed to prevent the ball from rolling out, a maneuver that has proven to be Walter Ray's greatest asset.

"C" Game: Straight Ball

The majority of players who opt for a "C" game normally resort to a straight ball, referred to as a *dart* or an *atom* shot: no hook, lots of speed, directly at the intended target. This shot is usually reserved for extremely dry conditions, single pin spares, or fill balls when no more than six pins are needed to ensure victory.

Remember these points when thinking about your own game:

☒ Versatility is the key to better bowling.

☒ The lanes dictate your strategy for success.

☒ Those who are best prepared to cope with the complications of varying lane conditions will reap the benefits.

☒ Develop your own alternative game plans.

11

Evaluating and Fine-Tuning Your Game

In all fields of sport, participants who strive for perfection—that is, those who seriously engage in their chosen sport—adhere to specific standards to maintain a competitive edge. They practice diligently, stay conditioned, and place their confidence in qualified coaches.

Practice

The old adage "practice makes perfect" can, at times, be an exaggeration. You may recall the old joke about the aspiring musician who was lost in New York City. He came upon a hippy and inquired, "How do you get to Carnegie Hall?" The hippy replied, "Practice, man, practice." Although practicing one's craft is a great work ethic and undoubtedly a worthwhile pursuit, it can be detrimental if it isn't done properly, particularly in bowling. Practicing your bowling is an absolute must. However, you must do it properly to derive any benefit to your game.

For example, when bowlers are focused and duplicating shot after shot, they are regarded as being "in the zone." They deliver quality shots with machinelike precision. They are undaunted by the prevailing

157

conditions—oily lanes, dry heads, wet-dry areas, hard-hooking back ends, slick or sticky approaches, or any other distractions that might otherwise affect their performances. However, bowlers who are in this kind of groove must never rest on their laurels and assume that the smooth path will continue unabated. Bowlers must maintain practice exercises regardless of how successful they are.

On the other hand, practice is not necessarily the panacea for those mired in a slump. Many bowlers whose games are on the decline labor under the delusion that the more they practice, the better they get. Contrary to this belief, I have subscribed to one basic conviction above all others: Repetition creates habits, good or bad.

Successful bowlers in the groove are executing properly and duplicating correct movements, so practice can only enhance their chances for continued success. Conversely, for those who are experiencing difficulty, rehearsing deficiencies that have crept into their games will only intensify and prolong their agony. They practice their mistakes so much, and they learn to make those mistakes so well, they can replicate them 9 out of 10 times in play. Don't keep practicing when what you need is help.

Consult a Knowledgeable Coach

Bowling, at its highest level, is an intricate sport. Unlike golf or tennis, seemingly great shots in bowling often result in negative results: 4-pins, 7-pins, 8-pins, or even gut-wrenching 10-pins. They can dishearten even the most resolute bowlers.

For example, high-pocket hits leave 4-pins; and with the advent of reactive bowling balls, 7-pin, 8-pin, and 9-pin stands have become increasingly visible. Modern hard-driving missiles have altered the course of normal shots. The stubborn 10-pin continues to be the bane of many high-average bowlers. This bugaboo has been further muddled by whistling hooks that enter the pocket at odd angles, thus perpetuating bowling's newest cliché, "pocket entry."

Actually, most 10-pins result from release flaws that are among the most difficult to detect with the naked eye. Basically, faulty release points lack the punch to carry the 10-pin. Unfortunately, only eagle-eyed bowlmasters can detect inferior release points. And those experts are precisely the people you should turn to for help in correcting your mistakes. That way, when you practice, you won't keep practicing bad habits.

To establish your goals, seek out a good coach or perhaps a teammate who understands your game. Go through all your motions and attempt

When you're experiencing difficulty in your game, seek out a good coach to help identify and correct mistakes.

to pinpoint areas of discomfort, loss of rhythm, and adjustments that have caused a liability in your game.

Maintain a Comfortable Style

One of the most important aspects of practicing is remaining natural. Do not become robotic. Many confused bowlers, hell-bent on perfection, often turn to books, gadgets, and programs that attempt to turn your game into a scientific model. These efforts create mechanical maneuvers and turn bowlers into automatons, particularly in clutch situations. Rigid deliveries usually produce chaotic results.

Be individualistic and execute in a matter that is comfortable for you. It is unwise to attempt to emulate someone else. However, you can learn

159

from other bowlers. If you share a similar style with a certain pro, you can study his technique for help in improving your own game. You can also learn from pros' mistakes. Whatever works for someone else won't necessarily work for you. For example, Marshall Holman stands in a crouch and has minimum backswing. He races to the foul line with four short steps, then, on his fifth step, slides about three feet, his slide continuing after the ball is released. Marshall's techniques work for him, but I don't recommend that anyone try to emulate them because they can prove disastrous.

Mark Roth is another bowler who has achieved success with an unorthodox style. He has amassed 34 titles with a rapid six- or seven-step approach, little knee bend, and a somewhat jerky snap release. Roth, with earnings well over a million dollars, bowled his way into the PBA Hall of Fame with a system far removed from the textbook style. Although Roth is credited with inspiring thousands of aspiring youngsters to adopt his thunderous release, no one on the pro tour and very few if any amateurs have attained any real success employing his unique style. On the other hand, stars such as Brian Voss, David Ozio, Mike Aulby, Parker Bohn III, and David Husted epitomize the smooth, classic style advocated by renowned coaches and bowling manuals everywhere.

Use Cameras to Detect Flaws

Serious bowlers should use video cameras to detect flaws and work out glitches that are impeding progress. This is especially recommended for those who have no access to a coach, but feel free to use cameras with or without instructional aid. Coaches with the keenness to detect minuscule flaws in a bowler's game are few and far between. Most proficient instructors favor cameras and slow-motion devices that allow for closer observation.

Practice Free From Distraction

In selecting time for practice, make certain you are able to isolate yourself from a crowded area. It is difficult to practice seriously with surrounding bowlers and noises that hamper your concentration. The majority of bowling centers have "off" times that might be better for practicing. If not, ask management to assign you lanes that are somewhat isolated from those in use.

Try to schedule practices when the lanes aren't crowded so you'll be free of distractions.

Focus on Correcting Weaknesses

In a legitimate practice, focus on correcting weaknesses. If the solid foundation and facets of your game have not deserted you, it is an exercise in futility to spend precious time on strong points that are still intact. Chances are, they are firmly entrenched in your game. Although it is wise to fine-tune them occasionally, it is more prudent to focus on your weaknesses. Seek them out and make adjustments that place you in a comfortable zone.

Are you comfortable in your stance? Do you feel a sense of discomfort as you stand and address the pins? If so, you are beginning the approach from a negative standpoint. Complete relaxation is a *must*. It is virtually impossible to perform well from a rigid position. The entire free-swinging process begins with a relaxed body.

Practice on Undoctored Lanes

Find a proprietor who will apply lane procedures that are not specifically dressed for high scores. Easy house conditions are not conducive to corrective measures in a flawed game, particularly where blocked conditions prevail. Practice sessions are totally unproductive when bowling balls automatically head for the pocket. If you are searching for solutions to your difficulties, you will benefit greatly from ethical lane conditions; they relay signals of flawed deliveries.

Practice sessions of serious bowlers are vastly different than those of recreational bowlers. Recreational bowlers engage in league play once or twice a week and generally use the game as a social function. They usually derive satisfaction from practicing fundamentals on doctored lanes that fail to disclose faulty execution. Other recreational bowlers practice to improve their averages. They take pride in leading their leagues in scoring statistics and are content to be big fish in small ponds. Then, of course, there are the top-rated amateurs who wield their talents in classic leagues that feature no-handicap scratch bowlers and teams. They vie for high-prize funds. Throughout the country, many league championship purses exceed $20,000.

Specifically, these bowlers are listed as amateurs, but in essence, they are professionals. Side pots and brackets run rampant in this bowling sphere. This arena of league bowling marks the difference between the recreational bowler and the "serious" bowler. Although high averages are a matter of pride, money winnings are the primary and controlling factor for this type of bowler. Bowlers in this classification possess the talent to join professional ranks and are categorized as serious bowlers. They practice their craft in earnest. Many of them rely on personal coaches for maintaining sharp games.

Unfortunately, there is another type of bowler: the sandbagger. These bowlers prey on legitimate bowlers in handicap tournaments. They literally steal in an undercover manner and, unlike bowlers who take great pride in achieving high averages, these bowlers intentionally post lower averages. Then they enter handicap tournaments and perform in clandestine by taking advantage of low-average players. The lower-average players participate in these tournaments because it gives them the opportunity to compete on their own level. Sandbaggers have been the bane of the game. They are unethical swindlers bereft of moral conscience and certainly sporting blood. They have been a source of irritation to the ABC, WIBC, and amateur tournament directors all over the country.

Regardless of who is practicing and why, make certain you are practicing the positive aspects of your game rather than using practice to reinforce the negatives of your game.

Physical Conditioning

Most professionals know that success in bowling not only requires practice on the lanes; it must include conditioning off the lanes. Amleto Monacelli, Brian Voss, Kim Adler and others too numerous to mention spend considerable time on physical conditioning. The most significant part of a bowler's body is the legs. The accepted belief is that once your legs go, so does your career. This applies to almost every sport: track, baseball, football, basketball, tennis, and yes, golf and bowling.

One of the prime examples of the importance of good legs can be found in the astounding exploits of Nolan Ryan, major league baseball's all-time strikeout artist and pitcher of more no-hitters than anyone in baseball history. The legendary Texan continued to blow away batters at age 43. He may have gone on for several more seasons if not for the years of wear and tear that took an irreversible toll on his magnificent arm. Ryan did, however, often attribute his longevity to his resolute and dogged leg conditioning.

Those who question the importance of proper leg conditioning can be comforted by the success of Ernie Schlegel, who, after turning 50, is enjoying a renewed career in bowling. The Vancouver, Washington, native carted off the PBA Touring Players Championship and the ABC Masters Championship at age 53. Both of these tournaments are of the long-format variety, which requires endurance. Not too surprising, Schlegel attributed his newfound energy to a sensible diet and a leg-conditioning program that includes running five miles daily. Schlegel, Voss, and Monacelli head a list of many players on the PBA tour who run daily to keep in condition.

Why do legs play such an important role in bowling? Simply put, legs are the foundation for upper-body balance. Legs control cadence in the approach. Proper knee bends eliminate deliveries from high positions that induce faulty release points and pulled shots.

Moreover, well-conditioned legs are the principal factor in extending the careers of athletes in every sport. In bowling, senior players Teata Semiz, Gary Dickinson, Johnny Petraglia, and Dave Soutar have remained competitive because of superb conditioning.

Many bowlers, like Kim Adler, recognize the importance of physical conditioning to success and longevity in the game.

Although weightlifting has become a regimen for athletes in many sports, it is not significant in bowling, Arm strength is an asset for endurance, free armswings do not depend on muscular forearms. In fact, the leaner the arm, the sweeter the swing. However, it is beneficial for bowlers to do exercises that strengthen the wrists.

For those who seek perfection in bowling, remember the hippy's sage advice to the lost, aspiring musician who wanted to know how to get to Carnegie Hall: "Practice, man, practice."

Slump Busting

Slumps beset individuals and teams in every field of sport. In baseball, such celebrated hitters as Willie Mays, Mickey Mantle, Stan Musial, Babe Ruth, and Pete Rose experienced brutal slumps during their careers. Similarly, all pitchers of renown have gone through agonizing periods of winlessness. Barring slumps, these superstars could have posted yearly batting averages of over .400 or recorded 30 victories every season. Even Michael Jordan, considered the greatest basketball player, experienced mild slumps, proving that he was mortal.

Professional golfers are more likely than most other athletes to slump. They are more susceptible because they must maintain control over so many facets of the game: driving off the tee, long irons, short irons, chipping, putting, and other maneuvers that depend on finesse and touch. Bowlers, like golfers, also rely on finesse and touch, so they too are more likely to encounter periods of decline.

What can occur to undercut the fruits of a bowler's hours of training in footwork, timing, release, follow-through, and balance? How can someone who has prepared a successful routine for scoring suddenly go bad? How can a bowler who has conquered fear, performed with supreme confidence, and achieved the heights of ambition unexpectedly plunge into the depths of depression?

Identifying the Cause

There are various causes for prolonged slumps, and there is no set of rules for correcting them. Consequently, a myriad of corrective measures can be applied for solving the different causes for a bowler's decline. A prime factor that prevents many bowlers from shaking a slump revolves around a bowler's physical makeup. The relationship between body shape and technique can be the source of a slump. For example, people with unusually long or short arms and legs or wider hips can't always successfully practice the same methods as those with more "ideal" physiques. In other words, you are trying things that work for others but you are physically unable to accomplish them in the manner you envision. Consequently, in the attempt to adjust, you can develop correcting faults that creep into your game and result in a slump. Slumps can have physical roots and are very difficult to discover and resolve.

Muscle memory is a key ingredient in all athletic endeavors. Pitchers who suddenly experience control problems or loss of movement on their fastballs, curves, and sliders often trace their failures to timing.

165

Timing is closely integrated with muscle memory. This fine-tuned mechanism is the spearhead for athletes who are on a roll. Any malfunctions that hamper the smooth flow of muscle memory can prove detrimental to successful execution, thus leading to a slump. And, with continued faulty execution, mental slumps become more prevalent.

It is little wonder, then, that every professional sports team hires specialized coaches with the experience and credentials to address the physical and the mental game. Baseball teams have hitting coaches, pitching coaches, and other specialized instructors. Football teams on all levels hire different coaches for different positions. Golfers, tennis players, track and field athletes are all under scrutiny of astute mentors.

Breaking the Slump

Fortunately, physical slumps can be corrected under the watchful eye of skilled instructors. Serious bowlers rely on personal coaches for corrective measures. Practically all PBA players who experience lapses in their game place their fortunes in the hands of a competent coach. With this said, it is wise to remember that bowling is rife with people who fancy themselves as competent instructors. Some of them prove to be more of a detriment than an asset. Results speak louder than words. Choose a coach with tried and true, as well as current, results.

Also, do not try to practice out of a slump without using camera work. A dedicated work ethic is imperative in filming yourself. It will take a lot of hard work and long hours of study. You may detect a flaw immediately through the magic of the cameras. For example, 10-pin stands are usually caused by poor entry angle. Poor entry angle can best be described as a strike ball that seemingly hits the pocket solid yet leaves the 10-pin. A closer view, perhaps in slow motion, will reveal the ball enters the pocket a fraction late and fails to generate a domino effect with the 3-6-10. A single 10-pin stand can reduce your score by as much as 10 to 30 pins. The pesky 10-pin stand can also be the result of too much speed or a weak release.

In those instances where you are hitting the pocket yet failing to strike, you might ask, "Why change anything when I'm hitting the pocket?" This is a valid question, but if you are not carrying the pins, there must be a flaw. This then becomes the arena for help from a coach. A proficient instructor can detect these flaws with the naked eye. Coaches who have studied the patterns of ball carry can remedy these situations by altering a player's rhythm, hand position, release point, speed, or follow-through or by enacting various other corrective measures.

When experiencing a slump, it's important to follow the advice of pros like Rick Steelsmith and check the basics to make sure your technique is sound.

Don't discount the fact that it may be necessary to start over. Check all the basics that were ingrained into your game: free armswing, foot patterns and cadence in the approach, hand position, release point, follow-through, and balance.

Many bowlers practice continually. Some succeed; some take off for a while. However, diehard bowlers never give up. They all take steps to return to form. As stated previously, there is no set pattern. Bowling instructional books merely serve to illustrate the basic fundamentals, and it is wise to remember that one method cannot apply to everyone. All bowlers should make every effort to use all avenues for the restoration of a previously successful game. On numerous occasions, when basic fundamentals failed to mend a bowler's game, I have dismissed teachings by the book and experimented with a variety of methods to achieve a result. I have exercised this freedom with numerous PBA players—Mike Aulby, Tim Criss, Robert Smith, Dave Husted, and Rick Steelsmith, to name a few.

Players who take their game seriously, particularly those sporting superior averages, are sometimes reluctant to seek help when mired in a slump. Many bowlers in the upper echelon of amateur competition have fragile egos. More often than not, they are reluctant to seek help. They attempt to work their way out of a slump rather than subject themselves to proper instruction. They may deem this as an affront to their prowess.

The smartest pros will set aside their pride and seek the help of a knowledgeable coach if their game happens to be suffering.

Professional players subscribe to a more perceptive theory. They are the best players in the world. They rely on performance for a living. They are bowlers that epitomize the essence of the sport. Unlike many amateur stars that are wrapped in a blanket of egotism and false security, most PBA stars' egos are built on perfection and pride in their chosen profession, and they readily seek help.

"When I'm experiencing a slump, I touch bases with the basics to be sure that my foundation is solid. Then, I seek help to identify what has gone out of kilter. I want to work on what is right with my game, not repeat a flaw. I also try to remember times that I bowled exceptionally well and how I felt then. I try to restore those positive feelings about my bowling. I also always try to remember to keep my breathing deep and natural. That seems to help my whole body relax. On occasion, while looking in a mirror, I have even resorted to talking to myself giving supportive dialogue."

Robin Romeo Mossontte
PWBA and WIBC Hall of Famer

Mike Aulby, Amleto Monacelli, Dave Husted, David Ozio, and Pete Weber have placed themselves among the immortals of the game. Yet they are not reluctant to seek the aid of coaches with proven reputations.

Pride becomes secondary to professionals who earn a living tossing 16-pound balls. Remember, find a good coach or instructor for shaking a slump in your physical game. Bowlers who seek to perform at the highest level must be willing to practice properly, maintain physical condition, and seek professional help when confronted with faulty execution.

12

Choosing Your Equipment

Serious bowlers seek all avenues to remain competitive. They stay abreast of all new equipment and pursue all means for elevating their games. During the past 10 to 15 years, the bowling game has undergone a technological phase. Bowling ball stock covers have been designed to improve the strike percentage for bowlers. Bowling shoes have been devised to improve the sliding process. Numerous wrist, arm, and finger supports have been created; some for the prevention of pain or injury, others for greater stability in their releases. All of these innovations have had a profound effect on the game.

Tailoring the Ball to Your Game

Bowling balls have evolved from the original wooden balls, to rubber, then polyester, urethane, reactive urethane, and Proactive urethane materials. During the early years of bowling, from the '20s to the late '50s, bowling balls were made of rubber. These balls were limited in scope yet unlimited in longevity. The average bowler used *one* ball for more than an entire league season, up to five years and even longer. Elite bowlers, particularly staff members of bowling ball companies and players of nationally sponsored teams, encountered little difficulty in acquiring new equipment. The average cost of bowling balls in the '40s

Serious bowlers carry an assortment of bowling balls to contend with differing lane conditions.

was under $18 and peaked in the late '50s at about $25. This was the golden age of the game—that is, an era that emphasized league play and team bowling.

Today, a top-caliber bowler may be content to carry four to seven balls in his or her arsenal: two for oily lanes; two for medium lanes; two for dry lanes; and one hard-surfaced ball, preferably a polyester ball, for spares. However, to be competitive in the 21st century, a bowler must have a complete arsenal: balls that hook at different lengths down the lane to maximize scoring. This can only be accomplished with balls that have different cores and shells.

172

High-average bowlers own at least 4 and as many as 30 balls. You can make each ball react differently by altering the shell, core, and method of drilling. Some balls will go long and flip hard on the back-end. Others will go long with a gradual arc on the back-end. Some are designed to hook early with a strong back-end, and others hook early with a smooth reaction on the back-end. Experience will tell you which ball to use to match up to different lane conditions for maximum striking power.

There are different variables that affect the ball's path. The radius of gyration (RG) determines how soon a ball hooks. The radius of gyration is a measurement of the ball's moment of inertia. The moment of inertia of a bowling ball is its resistance to revving up. The differential RG determines how much a ball can flare to create more friction with the lane. The shell material also affects the friction on the lane.

Polyester shells hook very little and are primarily used to pick up single-pin spares. Urethane shells create a medium amount of hook with a smooth arcing motion. A reactive shell causes the ball to slide in the oil and hook sharply on the dry back-end of the lane. Shells that contain particles create friction in the oiled area of the lane for more hook overall, especially in the front of the lane. Thus, serious bowlers need an assortment of balls to compete on all lane conditions they encounter. With top-of-the-line balls costing around $200, this can add up. However, many bowlers feel that the more balls they have to choose from, the less they will have to adjust their physical technique to create the shots they want. Although a wide range of bowling balls affords many options for scoring, some bowlers become flustered and confused with too many balls at their disposal. A few of the top players on the PBA tour carry fewer bowling balls and prefer to overcome difficult conditions by changing speeds and hand positions.

The Right Fit

The key is to select a ball that fits your hand and your game. The following are factors to take into consideration when fitting a bowler with functional grip:

- ☒ **Span**—the distance between the holes used for the purpose of grip
- ☒ **Pitch**—the angle at which the hole is drilled into the bowling ball
- ☒ **Hole size and shape**—the internal measurements and shape of the drilled inserts in the bowling ball

173

Two types of basic grips exist:

1. Conventional grip. The fingers are inserted to the second joint with the thumb seated in properly. The fingers will form a 90-degree angle when inserted into the holes. The conventional grip makes it easier to roll a straight ball but more difficult to impart rotation. This grip is popular with recreational bowlers.

2. Fingertip grip. In this grip, the fingers are inserted to the first joint. The thumb is seated in properly with the knuckle slightly raised from the ball. This should allow the first joint to stay in contact with the leading edge of the fingerhole so that the fingers form a 90-degree angle into the hole. This is the drilling method used by highly skilled bowlers. Fingertip grips make it easier to create rotation on the ball.

Ball-drilling experts take the following conditions into consideration when fitting a ball to a bowler:

☒ The length of the bowling hand determines the distance between the holes.

☒ The strength of the hand, wrist, and elbow is a factor in determining the proper weight of a bowling ball. Carpal tunnel syndrome, arthritis, and tendinitis must be taken into consideration.

☒ The flexibility of the hand and fingers plays a major role in determining pitch. As you grow older, flexibility decreases. Bowlers who work principally with their hands will experience different degrees of flexibility.

☒ Skin texture plays a role in diminishing pitch. Some hands are smooth and dry; others are rough and moist. Those with smooth and dry hands benefit from less reverse pitch or more forward pitch. Conversely, those with moist skin require more reverse pitch.

I suggest regular visits to a certified bowling technician at any bowling pro shop displaying the IBPSIA (International Bowling Pro Shop Instructors Association) logo. Certified bowling technicians can help fit you with the proper bowling ball.

Changes in hands and fingers can occur quickly. Ignoring proper grip adjustments may cause physical problems and adversely affect your bowling. According to internationally renowned bowling ball drilling expert and former president of IBPSIA Jerry Francomano, "No matter how good you are, you can't outbowl a bad fit."

The size of the hole is an important factor. Although a competent driller will concede on the size of the hole to somewhat patronize a bowler, rarely will he or she relent on span or pitch. Most skilled players prefer a tighter hole. Most bowlers use tape to adjust hole sizes to get the perfect feel, particularly in the thumbhole. Less-skilled players tend to use larger thumbholes and then apply and adjust tape to a smaller size. When the level of proficiency increases, they drill new balls.

A discussion on basic drilling patterns is included in this chapter, but I intentionally omitted all drilling techniques. Today's refined bowling balls, forged of ever-changing materials and built with sophisticated, strategically placed weight blocks, are packaged with drilling instructions. Pro shop operators stay abreast of all new innovations by attending drilling seminars sponsored by bowling ball manufacturers. The ever-changing patterns and techniques in modern ball construction render any of my drilling suggestions ineffectual. I urge you to choose an accredited, competent expert and rely on his or her judgment. I recommend the experienced services of any certified member of IBPSIA.

Determining the Best Ball Weight

The primary factors in selecting the right ball are your comfort in using the ball and the scoring ability of the ball. Most PBA bowlers use 16-pound balls, but many of them have dropped to 15-pound balls to minimize the effects of today's powerful missiles. Believe it or not, some players have even dropped to 14-pound balls. However, a 14-pound ball is more inclined to deflect off the head pin and not carry through the pocket. Therefore, a 14-pound ball is not advisable for those who can handle a heavier weight. At any rate, throw whatever weight feels comfortable, as long as the carrying percentage isn't seriously impaired.

There are no restrictions on minimum weight for bowling balls. In fact, most bowling ball companies make balls that range from 6 to 16 pounds. Balls in the 6- to 11-pound range are designed for children who gradually increase the weight as they grow older. Although most women in professional ranks use 15- to 16-pound balls, balls in the 12- to 14-pound range are the normal choice for women who engage in bowling on the recreational level.

The maximum weight for a bowling ball is 16 pounds. But 16-pound balls are normally manufactured with a gross weight of approximately

Basic Drilling Patterns

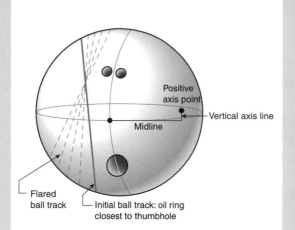

Figure 12.1 The positive axis point (PAP) for a right-handed bowler. A left-handed bowler would have the PAP on the left side of the grip, and the ball track would be on the right side. Therefore, drilling patterns for a left-hander are reversed.

Drilling experts customize ball drill patterns for each bowler by starting with the bowler's positive axis point (PAP). This is the location on the ball about which the ball initially rotates. The drilling expert finds this by determining the point on the ball that is equidistant from the initial ball track—that is, before the ball flares. This is the first oil ring on the ball and is the one closest to the thumbhole. For a three-quarter roller (ball track just outside of the fingers and thumb), the PAP is approximately 5 inches over from the center of the grip along the midline and a half-inch up along the vertical axis line. (See figure 12.1.) You can verify this by placing a piece of tape on the ball at this location. Have a friend observe your bowling. When the ball first comes off your hand and contacts the lane, the tape should spin in place without moving around the ball. It should appear stationary if it is on the PAP. The PAP for a left-handed bowler is on the left side of the grip. Therefore, a ball is drilled backward for a left-handed bowler.

Drilling patterns are techniques used to change the initial position of the core in the ball to alter its flare potential and the distance it travels down the lane before it starts to hook. Generally, more flare is equated to more hook because it increases the friction. You achieve this by keeping a dry area of the ball in contact with the lane instead of an oily area of the ball on the lane surface. Figure 12.2 shows how the flare potential and ball reaction change with different pin positions.

The pin position is important because it is the

Pins located 4½ to 6½ inches from PAP have reduced flare potential with more length and back-end reaction.

Pins located 3 to 4½ inches from PAP have maximum flare potential.

Pins located 1 to 3 inches from PAP have reduced flare potential and an earlier arcing ball reaction.

PAP

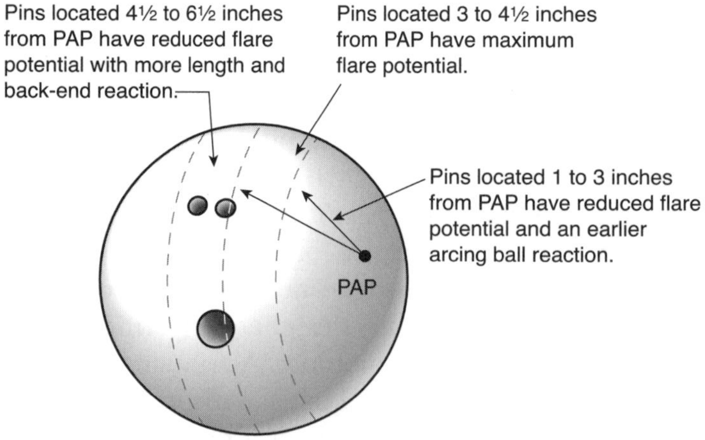

Figure 12.2 The flare potential and ball reaction of different pin positions.

The information on drilling patterns is provided by Jerry Francomano.

end of the core. By locating it at different distances from the PAP, we can create different motions from the same ball. The center of gravity (CG) is the heaviest point on the ball. Moving it to different locations has the same effect as moving the pin, but it has less impact on the pins.

For example, if a ball is drilled with the pin at 3 inches and the CG is at 1 inch, it will have maximum flare from the pin position. But, it will start hooking earlier with an arcing break point because of the CG position. The following describes the results and preferred conditions for various drilling patterns.

Early Hook With Flip Drilling

Pin to PAP distance	CG to PAP distance
3 $^3/_8$ to 4 inches	3 $^3/_8$ to 4 inches

Results—Creates track flare to give maximum friction between the ball and lane. Early break point and sharp turn.
Preferred lane condition—Best for oily lane conditions with and without carry-down.
Drawbacks—Can use up friction early, resulting in early rollout. Bowlers with an early roll style (12-15) may have their break point too early.

Early Roll With Arc Drilling

Pin to PAP distance	CG to PAP distance
3 $^3/_8$ inches	0 to 2 inches

Results—Arcing ball path. Will start hooking in oil, which will reduce the flipping motion at the break point. This drilling will require a dry back-end to allow the ball to finish.
Preferred lane condition:—Best for oily heads with some dry boards (for example, down the lane or outside).
Drawbacks—Carry-down on the back-ends will reduce the hitting power.

Extended Length With Strong Arc Finish

Pin to PAP distance	CG to PAP distance
5 to 6 $^1/_2$ inches	3 $^3/_8$ to 4 inches

Results—Minimum track flare to reduce the friction and get the ball farther down the lane to create the latest break point.
Preferred lane condition—Best for medium to dry lane condition and dry back-end. Will also perform well on second shift condition when the heads have dried up.
Drawbacks: May want to go too long and not flip enough on carry-down.
Caution—A pin shift of more than 6- 3/4 inches will cause the track to flare in the wrong direction (toward the thumbhole instead of away). Therefore, use caution when drilling the 6 and 6- 1/2-inch pin shift to ensure the pin to PAP distance is correct.

Label Drilling

Pin to PAP distance	CG to PAP distance
4 to 5 inches	near grip

Results—Will reduce the flip on the back-end, creating a strong, arcing back-end and an average distance to the break point.
Preferred lane condition—Fresh lane condition with oily heads and dry to medium back-ends. Will not overreact on back-end.
Drawbacks—Loses hitting power as the shot moves in deep because it does not have a strong back-end flip.

16 pounds, 2 ounces. The added 2 ounces compensate for the 2 or 3 ounces that are removed in the drilling process.

Two of the most noted professionals, Amleto Monacelli and Mike Aulby, use 15-pound balls instead of 16-pounders to minimize the hard-hitting effects. This was the philosophy credited to ABC Hall of Famer Dave Davis. He used 14-pound balls during the latter portion of his career. Many knowledgeable observers ascribe to this theory, particularly with the advent of modern hard-driving urethane balls. Nonetheless, the majority of players on the PBA tour continue to bowl with 16-pound balls.

Altering Ball Surfaces With Sandpaper

Bowlers can use sandpaper in a variety of grits to alter bowling balls slightly to meet the requirements for assorted lane conditions. Although ABC regulations prohibit the practice of forming a track in the ball with a foreign substance, it is permissible to sand the entire surface of the ball. Sandpaper is available in a variety of grits and, if properly applied, can profoundly affect ball reaction. Manufacturers are producing bowling balls with tremendous tracking surfaces, so many PBA players find the use of sandpaper increasingly unnecessary.

There are assorted grades of sandpaper; each grade provides a different reaction on the ball. However, one must use caution in applying sandpaper. Incorrect application of sandpaper may prevent restoration of the ball to its original state. The use of any grade of sandpaper under 400 grit greatly enhances the biting effect of the ball on the lanes. Bowlers who seek additional traction by applying grittier sandpaper run the risk of early hook and may experience the consequences of the rollout factor on dry back-ends. Although rollout can be overcome through the use of excessive speed, this strategy, in many situations, can profoundly hamper a bowler's rhythm and timing and be counterproductive.

Sandpaper can be used to apply a high-polish finish to a ball. A 600-grit paper is used for a medium to smooth finish, whereas grits in the 1,000 to 2,000 range are used for a high polish. On the other hand, Scotch-Brite® has become the most widely used product for removing the glaze on new balls. In fact, ingenious bowlers have mastered the art of Scotch-Briting the track in a ball to preserve the skidding effect in the early part of the lane yet maintain an advantage for traction in the hooking stage of the lane.

Advancements in Ball Material

Original bowling balls were made of wood. Wooden balls are no longer used, but they are on display at the International Bowling Hall of Fame and Museum in St. Louis. Rubber balls were originally made of pure rubber, but when the United States became involved in World War II in the early '40s, rubber became an important commodity for military use. Consequently, synthetic rubber became the alternative for civilian use. At that time, the most noted manufacturers of rubber balls in the United States were Brunswick®, Manhattan, Ace, and Ebonite®. Black was the primary color for male bowlers, but other colors in mottled designs were available, particularly for women and children.

During the late '50s, polyester balls were introduced. They featured sparkling colors but, more important, polyester balls displayed greater traction on the lanes, an advantage that provided higher scoring potential.

Polyester Balls

Before proceeding any further, I feel compelled to define *polyester*. All too often, bowlers use the word *plastic* to refer to polyester balls. This has been the most misused word in the bowling lexicon. The word *plastic* denotes a human-made concoction of various unnatural resins. The correct term is *polyester*. In the late '50s, polyester balls were produced and widely marketed by Brunswick and Columbia 300®, and soon after, they were manufactured by AMF, Ebonite, and Manhattan. Polyester balls eventually replaced rubber balls. They featured greater hooking traction and came in a variety of colors. The top price for multicolored polyester balls was $25.

In the early '70s, Don McCune devised a method for softening the shell of a bowling ball through the application of highly flammable chemical solutions, which combined methyl ethyl ketone and toluene. This chemical concoction softened the outer shell of the ball, a ploy that created greater tracking action on the lanes. The newfound magic transformed McCune from journeyman status to Bowler of the Year in 1973. McCune won five titles, became the leading money winner for the year, and gained recognition as the originator of the *soaker*. *Soaker* was the popular term used for balls that were soaked in a bucket of chemicals. Not long after, because of the volatility of these chemicals, the PBA was compelled to outlaw this practice.

Softer ball surfaces provided a desirable traction on the lanes, so Columbia 300 introduced the Sur-D bowling ball in 1974. It was a soft ball that registered less than 68 on the Shur-D Durometer. (The Shur-D Durometer is a device used to measure the surface hardness of a bowling ball. The Sur-D ball provided the greatest hooking traction of any ball ever made at that time. In fact, this ball dominated the 1974 ABC Masters tournament as no other ball in history had. No fewer than 15 of the top 16 finalists used the Sur-D ball. The soft surface of the Sur-D was far more susceptible to scratches and gouges and often showed indentations when placed on a ball ring in warmer weather. Bowlers, basking in the glory of newfound powers, simply ignored the marring effects and purchased new balls.

The Sur-D ball became so revolutionary, the American Bowling Congress instituted a regulation rendering all balls illegal that registered less than 72 degrees on the hardness scale. The Professional Bowlers Association went one step further by raising the hardness rule to 75. The new rule forced manufacturers to seek materials that met ABC standards yet provided bowlers with equipment that enhanced ball performance on the lanes. A short time later, Columbia 300 produced the Yellow Dot, a polyester ball that met the required 75-degree hardness rule yet had greater traction than any ball on the market. The Yellow Dot dominated the professional tour as no other ball and had a successful run for three or four years.

In 1974, John Fabovich, a ball designer, introduced the first bowling ball with a two-piece weight block in polyester material. It was the birth of Faball and, though the two-piece weight block had some redeeming qualities, it made little or no impact on the bowling ball industry—that is, at that time. Interestingly, Mr. Fabovich's concept was designed to create excess power in bowling balls. Weight blocks were placed in various positions within the ball that would enhance extra drive in the ball's path to the pocket. Mr. Fabovich's innovative creation would make a significant impact on the bowling ball industry in future years.

In 1976, a rubber ball with incredible traction characteristics made its mark on the PBA tour. It was designed by Louie Trier, a 48-year-old Brunswick engineer. Appropriately, it was named the Brunswick LT-48™. Within a year, Brunswick's superstar, Johnny Petraglia, endorsed the ball and it became the Johnny Petraglia LT-48. The LT-48 replaced the Yellow Dot as the most popular ball on the PBA tour and enjoyed a successful run through the '70s and early '80s.

Urethane Balls

In the early '80s, AMF introduced the Angle, the first urethane ball approved by the American Bowling Congress. Although the price of the ball seemed prohibitive ($89), it took the game by storm and practically eliminated other high-performance balls. The newly discovered urethane material exhibited greater traction on the lanes than any ball.

Skeptics expressed doubts about bowling balls that would retail for $89, but price did not stem the tide of record-setting sales of the Angle. Needless to say, other manufacturers followed suit, and elite bowlers rendered all other balls useless.

In the early '80s, John Fabovich sold Faball to two St. Louis bowlers, John Wonders and Earl Widman. Wonders and Widman began production of two-piece weight block balls with urethane materials. Faball realized instant success with a catchy brand name: the Hammer. The Hammer performed fairly well on the PBA tour in its original black color, but a short time later, Faball introduced the Blue Hammer, a ball that not only became the rage of the PBA tour but also the choice of elite bowlers all over the country until around 1989.

Reactive urethane balls. In late 1989, a California native, Steve Cooper, launched the Excalibur, a ball that provided the greatest tracking action of anything ever produced. This was the first ball featuring a reactive cover stock. Consequently, the word *reactive* crept into bowling jargon. *Reactive* describes the hooking ability of the ball. It creates greater friction on the lane and hooks more. Not surprisingly, within a year, every manufacturer jumped on the reactive ball bandwagon.

Proactive urethane balls. In the late '90s, Brunswick introduced a Proactive ball constructed of urethane resins containing gritty particles. The gritty contents enabled the ball to literally claw into the lanes and create a greater hooking effect. Naturally, all other manufacturers followed Brunswick's lead, and *Proactive* became another word in the bowling vernacular.

Although new innovations in bowling ball materials created greater traction on the lanes and provided bowlers with a clear advantage for striking percentage, the new materials caused trouble for lane maintenance crews worldwide. The greater oil absorption of urethane balls, caused by their porosity, literally ate up lane dressings. Porosity indicates the softness or the absorbency of a given material and is the determining factor for coefficient of friction. As mentioned previously, the softer or more abrasive the shell of the ball, the lesser the skid factor, thus providing an increase and advantage of traction and the greater possibility for increased scoring.

Although most of the skyrocketing scores are a result of doctored lane conditions, the American Bowling Congress and the Women's International Bowling Congress have taken further steps to control the scoring madness by sanctioning the revision of two important specifications on all bowling balls. In early 2001, the ABC's and WIBC's Equipment Specifications Committees approved the tightening of the upper-average specifications of the friction coefficient of bowling balls (from .39 to .32). The revision applies to any new ball or the remanufacture of any previously approved ball. Any bowling ball currently approved will remain on the approved ball list. These figures apply solely to bowling ball manufacturers. They also place a limit on the porosity factor allowed in all future manufacturing specifications and therefore will somewhat limit the hooking ability.

Unbelievable as it may seem, modern bowling balls for the elite players are priced in the $210 to $225 range. New balls are being introduced at a monthly rate, each featuring a variety of claims of supremacy. But, there is no built-in magic in any ball. Proper execution will inevitably overcome any cover stock, weight block, pin placement, or other claims.

Selecting the Right Shoe

When it comes to footwear, you have a choice between renting and buying. Rental shoes are a staple in bowling centers for the convenience of occasional recreational bowlers. But rental shoes have two sliding soles, rather than one sole for sliding and one for braking, which means that they are not conducive to good bowling. Rental shoes merely fill the need for those who are not serious about the game. Your best bet is to invest in a good pair of shoes that matches your bowling style and can handle a variety of approach conditions.

Atmospheric conditions can seriously affect approaches. Weather influences lane patterns and also affects approaches. Bowlers must contend with slippery approaches that hamper braking while other approaches become tacky and prevent a smooth slide. Because of this, professional bowlers place as much, if not more, faith in bowling shoes as they do in bowling balls.

Pro players, like Chris Barnes, recognize the importance of having shoes that can handle a variety of approach conditions.

"Bowling shoes are so much better today because they give you so many variations. These days you bowl on lighter wood or synthetic approaches and they slide differently. Then you have the humidity factor, high or low, which also affects sliding conditions. Bowling is a sport like any other sport. If you want to play it well, you have to go out and buy the very best equipment for your game. Spending $30 on a pair of shoes is not going to help your game."

Johnny Petraglia
PBA Hall of Famer and senior tour member

183

Today's high-performance bowling shoes offer interchangeable heels and soles designed to alter sliding and braking patterns to adjust to any approach condition. Removable soles, heels, and inserts are beneficial features of bowling shoes. However, they are not an absolute *must* for all bowlers who take the game seriously. The principal objective to correct sliding is to make certain the sliding sole is constructed of smooth leather. The opposite shoe sole should be built of soft rubber.

Although the majority of bowlers are content with conventional heels, a raised or lowered heel height can also regulate sliding patterns. A raised heel lessens the slide; a lowered heel increases it.

The majority of PBA and high-level amateurs place extreme importance on the sliding soles of their shoes. Consequently, to maintain clean sliding soles and avoid any mishaps in sliding patterns, they include a wire brush among their accessories.

> *"In the old days, we worried about the sliding foot, but now we know that we must also have the best shoe possible on the pushaway foot. With these new combinations, you can create sticky soles (on the nonsliding foot), which can give you good leverage at the foul line."*
>
> *Earl Anthony*
> *PBA and ABC Hall of Famer and six-time Player of the Year*

Improvements in Footwear

From the '30s to the '50s, when bowling balls lasted many seasons, bowling shoes lasted perhaps 10 years, depending on the amount of use. Like most modern bowling shoes, they had a leather sole for sliding and a rubber sole for braking. They sold for up to $10 a pair.

Bowling shoes have undergone tremendous changes since the '30s and '40s. During the '30s, the Jimmy Smith brand was the choice of top bowlers. It was constructed of high-quality leather and sold for less than $10. The desire to create shoes that can contend with varying lane conditions and meet the needs of bowlers with different styles has led to constant improvements in footwear. During the '40s and '50s, Hyde bowling shoes were the choice of better bowlers. There was one exception, however: Lind custom-made shoes. The sliding ability of Lind shoes, along with their unique red kidskin material, revolutionized the game. Top-rated players chose Lind shoes that had to be special ordered and necessitated premeasurements. Today, Lind shoes are displayed in pro shops all over the United States.

The Lind Shoe Story

The Lind shoe story reads as a Horatio Alger novel. In 1919, Leslie Lind and his father, Erick, had a small shoe shop in St. Paul, Minnesota, that made shoes for the wealthy railroad and lumber industry executives. They also made ice skates and dancing slippers. One day in 1936, a man from Hamm's Brewery came to the shop. The gentleman was a member of the Hamm's bowling team and wanted to know whether Mr. Lind had anything that would slide. Lind had a piece of buckskin and agreed to attach a piece of this material to the sole of the bowling shoe. The next day, the man returned with the rest of the team and wanted to outfit all of them. Lind said he could make a shoe that would serve the sport better than what was available at the time and offered to make shoes for the team. The team liked the idea but wanted something that would really stand out. Before this, Lind designed dancing shoes made of red kidskin for a Ukrainian dance troupe. Lind used this material for the Hamm's team's shoes. The team members loved them and used them in a match against the Stroh's Beer team in Detroit. Shortly after this match, the Stroh's team called Lind and requested the same shoes. Stroh's purchased the new red kidskins every year after that, except for the war years.

In 1941, Lind joined the armed services and closed the shop. After returning from the war, he began making special shoes for the Veterans Administration. He found the work rewarding because without these shoes, many of the disabled veterans would not have been able to walk. Knowing the VA business had its limitations and would soon make their own shoes, he continued to make a few bowling shoes. The demand for bowling shoes became so great that bowlers had to wait weeks, sometimes months, to receive the made-to-fit shoes that sold for $45 to $60, a rather exorbitant cost at that time.

In 1968, Leslie Lind's son, Jeff, joined the firm. During his early years with the company, Jeff answered the phone and mail and had the opportunity to speak with many bowlers. He learned a great deal about the bowling business and thought that changes in business policy were necessary. Orders were piling up. They were 18 months behind and something had to be done. In 1970, Lind Shoes moved to Stillwater, Minnesota, a town 20 miles east of St. Paul. They occupied an old abandoned shoe factory and invested in new equipment, and things started to look good—so good, in fact, they were opening the mail in the morning and making the shoes that afternoon.

In 1976, Lind wrote to his 10 best customers (pro shops) and offered them shoes available in stock sizes, white, D width only, with a minimum order of 12 pairs. Today, Lind features shoes in every size and color, plus interchangeable soles and heels, all designed to meet each bowler's needs.

Dexter began making bowling shoes in 1961 and is now one of America's largest shoe manufacturers. They entered the high-performance bowling shoe market in 1988 when they introduced the SST™ line of shoes and hired David Ozio as their PBA representative. Ozio and other professionals recommended various designs and styles, including the SST3, SST4, and SST5. The SST3 shoe made it possible to alter the power pivot sole for the nonsliding shoe. The SST4 had interchangeable soles to alter the slide, and the SST5 not only had interchangeable soles but also interchangeable heels. Dexter advertisements feature attachments and removals of assorted Velcro inserts designed to change sliding and braking patterns in 16 different combinations. These shoes are priced in the $150 range.

> *"I don't think the league bowlers, not even the good ones, realize how important the bowling shoe is to their game. If a bowler starts leaving a weak 10 or if his or her bowling ball is hitting flat, they may not be getting good leverage and it's time to try a new sole or inserts."*
>
> *John Handegard*
> *14-time senior titlist and Senior Player of the Year in 1991, 1995, and 1996*

Although Lind and Dexter have revolutionized the interchangeable soles, heels, and inserts, this innovative concept must be credited to Riedell Shoes of Red Wing, Minnesota. Riedell specialized in the production of ice skates and had numerous outlets, particularly for hockey skates. In the early '50s, Paul Riedell received a call from Max Lubin, proprietor of a sporting goods store in Massachusetts. Lubin specialized in hockey and bowling equipment. Riedell recommended a bowling shoe with removable ovals in the center of the sole. It was called the Joe McCord bowling shoe. Somehow, the Riedell concept did not have the impact on bowlers of that era as today's sophisticated bowling shoes do.

Bowling Accessories

Several accessories, including bags, hand and wrist supports, grips, inserts, towels, and skin treatments, help enhance bowlers' games.

Bowling Bags

Bowling bags have undergone significant changes over the past 20 years. During the '70s and '80s, Triangle and Colonial bags were the choices of elite bowlers. Each featured metal frames to secure balls and ample space below to store shoes. These bags also provided space for other accessories.

Bowling bags come in all sizes and shapes. Recreational bowlers can purchase one-ball bags that provide space for one pair of shoes. They are available at pro shops as well as sporting goods and department stores. Two-ball bags are also available at department stores.

In the late '80s, ball manufacturers commissioned companies in Korea and Taiwan to produce the most sophisticated bowling bags imaginable. Bags were built to hold two, three, and four balls with ample space for shoes and accessories. These bags functioned as luggage, complete with wheels. They also became costlier. Professionals and top amateurs carry three or more luggage-type bags to store their equipment. PBA players are restricted to eight balls at a time in the locker area, which is an excessive amount, considering the limited space allotted in the players' area at most bowling centers.

Hand and Wrist Supports

Various wrist, arm, finger, elbow, and forearm devices have flooded the market; all are designed or purported to aid in shot execution. They are more noticeable among professional female bowlers. Carolyn Dorin-Ballard, Kim Adler, Wendy Macpherson, and Aleta Sill all wear wrist supports.

It is interesting to note that superstars Parker Bohn III, Norm Duke, Chris Barnes, Amleto Monacelli, and Walter Ray Williams shun performance-enhancing gadgets. Nonetheless, Jason Couch, Tim Criss, Bob Learn, and Ryan Shafer sport either wrist, hand, or arm supports to execute quality shots.

One of the more unusual accessories is a glove worn by Pete Weber. It is built similar to a golfer's glove; that is, it covers the hand. However, Weber uses this glove solely as a protection for his fingers. It has no affect on his game whatsoever.

Although some hand and wrist supports appear to be cumbersome and uncomfortable, they have proven beneficial to many bowlers and particularly helpful to some female bowlers. Basically, many wrist supports are devised to prevent the breaking back of the wrist, thereby ensuring a firmer release. Nevertheless, some of the greatest releases among top-rated bowlers feature a broken-back wrist with a rapid forward acceleration. This is discussed in detail in chapter 5.

Many professional female bowlers, including Wendy Macpherson, wear wrist supports to aid in their release.

Several years ago the splint, a forearm support, was introduced to the bowling world. The splint is a device consisting of thin straps worn around an area from the wrist to the elbow. The splint was designed as preventive maintenance for tendons in the forearm. This innovation was very helpful for six-title pro Roger Bowker. Bowker has an unusual stance wherein he extends the ball with his right arm rested against his

188

hip, a position that places extreme strain on the forearm. After sustaining strained tendons in his forearm, Bowker began using the splint. He derived great satisfaction from this device and, although he no longer wears the splint, it prolonged his career.

Wrist, hand, and arm accessories are a matter of preference. In many cases, they have become a mental comfort. Also, on the professional level, it is a source of income for players who endorse these products. Whether they enhance a player's performance is debatable. For example, years ago, a major glove manufacturer formed an advisory staff. The staff signed a group of top-name stars on a monthly retainer fee. The principal feature of this glove was a padded palm that placed the ball firmly in the hand. Nevertheless, one of the top players on the star-studded staff removed the palm pad and simply wore the glove. It merely covered his hand and fingers and had absolutely no effect on his release. When asked if the gadget helped him, he simply replied without hesitation, "Yeah, about $100 a month."

Tape

Thumbs and fingers are prone to shrinking or swelling, causing difficulty in gripping or releasing the ball. Tape has become the greatest adjuster and modifier as a quick fix to fit a favorite ball. Tape comes in several textures; adhesive and plastic are the most commonly used. Each can be of great advantage. Adhesive tape can delay the exiting of the thumb or fingers. On the other hand, plastic tape, with a slicker composition, promotes instant exiting of either fingers or thumb and acts as a deterrent for hanging in the ball.

Adhesive tape, similar to medical tape, is courser and affords a greater gripping advantage than plastic tape does. It is applied on the front area of the thumb to achieve two purposes:

1. It prevents the bowler from squeezing the ball out of fear of dropping it in the backswing. In this manner, a bowler can exercise a relaxed swing.

2. It provides a firmer grip in the thumb, a tactic that simplifies shifting the ball weight from the thumb to the fingers at the release point. Although this statement seemingly conflicts with the slower releasing characteristic of adhesive tape, it must be noted that the thumb has arrived at the release point in a flat plane, and the transferring of the weight from the thumb to the fingers is simplified through the freeing of the thumb grasp.

I firmly advocate the natural, rapid exit of the thumb, particularly for bowlers with flexible hands. Consequently, I do not recommend adhesive tape on the back part of the thumb. I would suggest plastic tape for the back of the thumb because it forms a slicker surface and permits the thumb to exit unimpeded.

Grips and Inserts

Many professional and top amateur bowlers place as much importance on thumb and finger inserts as they do on drilling configurations. Unbeknownst to many contemporary players, inserts were in vogue during the '40s. Inserts were popular among many bowlers, particularly players who were accustomed to using tape to assure a stronger grip in the ball.

The original inserts were made in various sizes for thumbs and fingers. They were called *ovals*. Unlike modern inserts, they did not necessitate drilling and were sold in various sizes. Sometime between the late '40s and the late '50s, oval inserts disappeared. Also, during this era, Manhattan Rubber Company, a leading manufacturer, formulated a ball with a soft rubber texture just below the surface of the ball. The softer material, approximately one-quarter inch below the outer surface, provided a slip-free grip.

During the late '30s or early '40s, Ace Mitchell introduced Ace Mitchell Shur-Hooks. These inserts, shaped like modern tape inserts, were made of cork material and were ridged for firmer gripping. Sur-Hooks dominated the market and were used by almost every elite bowler. Sur Hooks were still in demand until the early '70s and, although they gave way to modern inserts, they are still an important item in bowling pro shops.

In the early '60s, Steve Vesarakis, a Californian, invented the Pro Grip, a solid insert of clear material. In 1961, Don Heimbigner of Vancouver, Washington, bought the product and moved it to Vancouver. The company became known as Don's Sports Systems, then it changed to Pro Sports Systems. The inserts became known as Contour Power Grips.

Although the clear material did not catch the fancy of the bowling public, it was in compliance with the ABC. The ABC was mandated to prevent cheaters and hustlers from inserting lead below the surface of the ball, a deceptive ploy that jeopardized the integrity of the game. In 1978, Heimbigner met Ernie Schlegel and appointed him as sales representative on the PBA tour. To Schlegel's credit and salesmanship, grips were resurrected and have become a major force in the modern bowler's arsenal. In fact, numerous others became involved in the grip business, such as Turbo 2-N-1 and Vise Grips.

Bowling Towels

Bowling towels have become an essential commodity in a bowler's accessory bag. Bowling balls absorb oil on freshly conditioned lanes, and towels are particularly useful for removing oil tracks. Additionally, they have become useful advertising vehicles for bowling ball manufacturers that design towels with logos that are clearly visible not only to the crowds in attendance but particularly on men's and women's pro bowling telecasts. Nevertheless, towels have become such a fixation and obsession that many bowlers wipe off bowling balls when lanes are practically oil-free. Many accessories serve as mental consolations.

Skin Treatments

Bowlers, particularly those that apply excessive effort in executing shots, often experience sore thumbs. Although most PBA strokers are not as susceptible to thumb and finger problems as other types of bowlers, they can nonetheless be affected by the rigors of delivering 16-pound bowling balls repeatedly day after day and week after week during qualifying and match play rounds and many hours of practice. Crankers are particularly vulnerable to sore thumbs. For example, Mark Roth's bowling thumb is considerably larger than his other thumb because of his vigorous release.

It is safe to assume that the majority of skin treatments are derived from the same sources as the original skin treatment, colodian, a nitrocellulose solution that dries into a tough, elastic film used to protect wounds. The most popular brand among elite players is Robby's Skin Protector. Other skin treatments are available in pro shops, but they are all essentially colodian related.

Accessories play an important role in a bowler's arsenal. Each accessory has its purpose and each should be incorporated as needed in a bowler's game. But remember, what is good for one bowler is not always good for everyone. Nonetheless, the most important equipment for high performance is a properly fitted bowling ball. Bags, wrist and hand supports, tape, sandpaper, and skin treatments can enhance a bowler's game, but the only offensive weapon for knocking down pins is a ball that fits comfortably, comes off the hand cleanly, and is released out on the lane with no difficulty. Simply seek the services of a certified bowling technician at any bowling pro shop bearing the International Bowling Pro Shop Instructors Association label.

191

13

Competing Successfully in Leagues and Tournaments

There are four ways to play the sport of bowling: league, open play, tournament, and elite. The great thing about bowling is that it can be played at any level, as a recreational activity or as a competitive sport.

Bowling provides endless social and competitive opportunities. There is the camaraderie of being part of a team as well as the opportunity to attain personal goals, such as the first 600 series, then the first 700, and, of course, the first 300 game.

League Bowling

League bowling has been the backbone of the sport since the ABC (American Bowling Congress) formed in 1895. People form teams of two, three, four, and five players that compete on a regular basis for a specific period of time. Leagues set some form of competitive schedule in which champions are crowned at the end of the season, usually at a bowling banquet.

League bowling is a tremendous experience. It's a chance to get away from the pressures of daily life and to relax and have fun with friends and family. Nearly all pro bowlers began their bowling careers by engaging in league play. Children from three years up are taught the game in Learn to Bowl classes. They advance into junior leagues and eventually into adult leagues that feature team play.

League participation is a group of people sharing a common interest: the desire to compete regularly in bowling. Many times, it involves competing with coworkers or friends from the same church or club. Leagues can consist of as few as 4 teams to as many as 50. A team is composed of two, three, four, or five bowlers. There are mixed leagues, senior leagues, all men, all women, and any combination thereof. Most important, there are leagues for every ability, thanks to a handicap system.

Leagues can be scheduled during the morning, afternoon, evening, weekdays, or weekends. One of the great features of league bowling is the various divisions of competition. Top-caliber bowlers usually compete in nonhandicap leagues, generally referred to as classic leagues but, aside from scratch leagues, the proven handicap system provides less-talented players the opportunity to bowl on the same team with the top performers in an area.

Decline of Team Bowling

Five-man team bowling, a form of league bowling, has gradually declined during the past 35 years. This is principally due to the PBA's tremendous impact on individual competition beginning in the early '60s. Before the '60s, bowling on a great team was the goal of every aspiring bowler in America. Team bowling offered the excitement of competition at the city, state, and national level.

Team bowling on the national level reigned supreme before the organization of the Professional Bowling Association in the early '60s. Teams from Chicago, Milwaukee, Detroit, Cleveland, St. Louis, and the New York-New Jersey areas fielded teams with star-studded line-ups, many of whom became ABC Hall of Famers. Budweiser, Falstaff, Strohs, Hamm's, Pfeiffer's, Meister Brau, and Monarch were staunch supporters.

Teams made up the strongest leagues in bowling history and annually competed in the Bowling Proprietors Association of America (BPAA) All-Star Championships. However, with the emergence of the PBA, team bowling lost its appeal. Budweiser superstars Don Carter, Dick Weber, Ray Bluth, and Bill Lillard, plus Falstaff members Billy Welu, Harry Smith,

Dick Hoover, and Glen Allison all opted for the PBA and the glory of individual performances in the professional game.

In recent years, the ABC has conducted the World Team Challenge Championships. Regional tournaments are conducted throughout the country to qualify winners that compete against one another in a finals championship at the end of the year. The format in the finals is based on the Baker system of scoring. This is a format designed by Frank Baker, the late executive secretary of the ABC. Baker originated this scoring method for FIQ (Federation Internationale dea Quilleurs, or International Bowling Federation) tournaments.

The Baker system puts a greater emphasis on the team concept and practically eliminates individualism in the sport. Each bowler bowls one frame, with the lead-off player bowling the first and fifth frame, the second bowler the second and sixth, and so on. The anchorman has the opportunity to bowl two additional frames, the 11th and 12th, providing he or she strikes. The Baker system is widely employed in collegiate bowling as well as in a majority of team scoring in FIQ international play.

Average and Handicap

There is a mistaken belief that to be a league bowler you must average 180 or better. Quite the contrary. The median average for men is 163 and for women about 137. Bowling has developed a nearly perfect handicap system, which makes it possible for bowlers of varying degrees to compete on an equitable basis. You can be a member of a team no matter what your average is.

The league sets a "par" figure higher than the known ability of the best bowler in the league. For example, if the highest bowler has an average of 176, the figure should be at least 180. A percentage of handicap also is set. A 100 percent handicap is the most equitable system. The lower the handicap percentage, the more advantage the higher-average teams and individuals have. For example, a 90 percent handicap usually results in closer results than 80 percent handicap. Each bowler's handicap is determined by subtracting his or her average from par and multiplying by the percentage established.

Let's say you have a 130 average and you join a league where the highest average of a person in that league is 180. The handicap percentage in that league is 90 percent. Therefore, subtract 130 from 180, which leaves 50. Then take 90 percent of 50, resulting in 45 pins. Thus, 45 pins are added to your score in competition each game.

Each week the league publishes and distributes a standing sheet, giving every bowler's actual average as well as team standings and high game and series.

How to Organize or Join a League

Bowling league organization begins with a meeting to which all prospective members are invited. It can be held at a bowling center, public meeting place, or even at a bowler's home. Members should elect a president, vice president, secretary, and treasurer or a combination of the latter two. At the first meeting, members should elect team captains because they make up the league's board of directors with the officers. Team members also can be assigned, or each captain can organize his or her own team.

Before league organization is completed, you should elect a committee of two or three members to meet with the bowling center manager so that they can discuss the issues that relate to your leaque. These issues can include price per game, day and time for the league, number of weeks in the schedule, number of lanes needed, size of teams, and the policies that the bowling center and your league would like to adhere to.

If you would like to join an already-established league, you should contact either a bowling center or the local bowling association. They will be glad to put you in touch with leagues that need bowlers. All league bowlers should strive to have their leagues sanctioned. League bowling is enjoyed within the framework of organized competition by the sport's governing bodies:

☒ **ABC**—The American Bowling Congress regulates men's and mixed leagues and oversees the collegiate program in conjunction with the WIBC.

☒ **WIBC**—The Women's International Bowling Congress regulates women's and mixed leagues and oversees the collegiate program in conjunction with ABC.

☒ **YABA**—The Young American Bowling Alliance regulates youth bowling.

These organizations were founded to preserve the integrity and foster the enjoyment of the sport so that members can derive satisfaction from their league and tournament experience.

Membership dues support these organizations, which provide many services including awards, rules, league supplies, publications, tournaments, manuals, bonding of league funds, educational seminars, and testing equipment specifications. These organizations are also a ready reference for questions.

Open Play

Open play consists of unorganized or organized bowling games. Unorganized open play can mean friends rolling a couple of games on the spur of the moment. Children can go with their parents or couples can go bowling on a date. Or someone simply may want to practice either alone, with a coach, or with one or two others who can offer analysis and critique. However, when you practice with friends, you must only take advice from competent bowlers or coaches who know the game and are familiar with your bowling style. Unfortunately, bowlers are subject to the old adage "too many cooks spoil the broth." Bowling, like many other individual sports, is replete with wanna-be coaches whose comments are well intended but unfounded. Although practice is the key to improving and advancing your game to another level, it is beneficial only when applied properly.

Organized open play includes activities such as birthday parties, company outings, "glow bowling," or rock 'n' roll bowling.

Tournament Bowling

Tournament bowling is a more organized activity where competition is at its fiercest. These events can take place over one day, one weekend, one month, or several months. They range from in-center competitions to city, state, regional, national, and international championships where medals are awarded. People place equal importance on the yearly city and state tournaments that determine champions in all categories. The most significant nonprofessional tournaments in the United States are the annual ABC and WIBC Championship Tournaments. These are contests to determine the top performers in team, doubles, singles, and all events. These annual tournaments are reserved for amateurs. They are held at the National Bowling Stadium in Reno every third year for the ABC and WIBC. In the other two years, they are held in communities that are chosen several years in advance.

In the men's division, touring professionals are not permitted to bowl. Regional players and nontouring players can participate in the annual

ABC tournament. Each team is permitted two nontouring pros. PBA touring players interested in maintaining an ABC record and establishing an average can do so by performing in the annual ABC Masters Tournament. There are four divisions of competition in the WIBC national tournament:

Open division:	180 average and over
Division 1:	165 to 179 average
Division 2:	150 to 164 average
Division 3:	149 and under average

In the open division of team play, WIBC rules allow two professionals per team. In the doubles, only one pro bowler is permitted.

Elite Bowling

Elite bowling can be broken down into two categories: professional and amateur. A professional in sport is a person who either earns a living performing and competing in the sport or earns as much money in the game as he earns in his chosen profession.

Men in the PBA and ladies on the PWBA (Professional Women's Bowling Association) tour are card-carrying professionals and have declared their status. However, numerous bowlers in the United States and around the world prefer to maintain amateur status, but in reality, they bowl for a living. I refer to these types of bowlers as *closet professionals*. They qualify for all amateur tournaments, including the BPAA (Bowling Proprietors' Association of America), U.S. Open, the ABC Masters, all megabucks tournaments, all FIQ tournaments, and a slew of high-paying tournaments around the world that are closed to card-carrying PBA and PWBA players. These amateurs are ever-present at all High Roller and Eliminator tournaments and enter practically all brackets and sweepers. Usually pro amateurs do not win the grand prize but take the bulk of the money in brackets and sweepers.

Many of these so-called amateurs earn as much as any leading professional and much more than most touring pros. Nonetheless, elite bowlers who are not among the pro amateur category enjoy competing for spots on team USA. Team USA offers members of the ABC, WIBC, and YABA the opportunity to represent their country in international competition.

It takes exceptional skill, determination, and perseverance to make it
on the pro tour.

Bowling's Governing Body

Bowling is the largest organized sport in the world. About 80 million
people visit bowling centers yearly, and the unofficial number of organized bowlers is around 5 million. As a rule, all organizations require
regulations. The ABC, the governing body of organized bowling since
1895, is responsible for maintaining the standardization of the game

through its specifications for equipment. (The WIBC has had joint responsibility for standardization with the ABC since the mid-'80s.) ABC and WIBC conduct annual lane inspections to certify compliance with specifications.

The ABC and WIBC set rules for the game and provide guidance on rules for leagues and tournaments. They also provide a court of appeals where disputes and rules problems can be referred for review, council, and decision if the need arises. Among other things, the ABC and WIBC provide awards in bowling, automatic bonding coverage insurance for more than $175 million every season, sanctioning service to more than 10,000 tournaments every season, and materials essential to every league. But, most important, ABC and WIBC preserve the integrity of the sport!

Today, more than 80 million people visit bowling centers throughout North America at least once a year. Bowling is one of America's most popular sports, but more important, it is one of the most organized. Nearly four million adults and youths participate regularly in sanctioned leagues throughout North America. Bowling is not only enjoyed in North America. It has progressed rapidly in Central America, South America, Europe, Asia, and Australia. It is played in more than 80 countries worldwide and is recognized by the United States Olympic Committee and as a medal sport at the Pan American Games. It is one of the few sports in which grassroots participants can qualify for international competition.

Appendix:
Pro Players John Jowdy Has Coached

PBA

Rich Abboud

Bryan Alpert

Mike Aulby

Mark Baker

Del Ballard

Bob Benoit

Joe Berardi

Parker Bohn III

George Branham

Allie Clarke

Paul Colwell

Steve Cook

Tim Criss

Tom Crites

Darrel Curtis

Tommy Delutz

Scott Devers

Dale Eagle

Frank Ellenberg

Tommy Evans

Dave Ferraro

Joe Firpo

Paul Fleming

Eric Forkel

Don Genalo

Jeff Germann

John Handegard

Bob Handley

Patrick Healey

David Husted

Marshall Holman

Steve Hoskins

Tommy Hudson

Don Johnson

Jack Jurek

Rudy Kasimakis

Steve Kloempken

Paul Koehler

Larry Lichstein

Jeff Lizzi

Pete McCordic

Marc McDowell

Sam Maccarone

Tim Mack

Steve Martin

John Mazza

Amleto Monacelli

Jeff Morin

Rowdy Morrow

Warren Nelson

Andy Neuer

David Ozio

Ron Palombi

George Pappas

Randy Pedersen

Johnny Petraglia

Phil Prieto

Jimmy Pritts

Ed Richardson

Phil Ringener

Jay Robinson

Mark Roth

Joe Salvemini

Carmen Salvino

Ernie Schlegel

Teata Semiz

Mike Shady

Robert Smith

Bill Spigner

Jess Stayrook

Rick Steelsmith

Bret Sterley

Gene Stus

Bill Swanson

Charlie Tapp

Brian Voss

Kent Wagner

Lonnie Waliczek

Chris Warren

Del Warren

Wayne Webb

Pete Weber

Derek Williams

Steve Wilson

Danny Wiseman

Rich Wolf

Steve Wunderlich

PWBA

Donna Adamek

Debbie Ayers

Alayne Blomenberg

Pam Buckner

Paula Carter

Tori Romeo Carter

Cheryl Daniels

Anne Marie Duggan

Nikki Gianulias

Vesma Grindfels

Lilia Johnson

Tish Johnson

Millie Ignizio Martorella

Pat Mercatanti

Betty Morris

Kelly Morrow

Robin Romeo Mossontte

Aleta Sill

Lisa Wagner

Index

Note: The italicized *f* following page numbers refers to figures.

About the Author

Courtesy of Bowlers Journal International

John Jowdy is a legend in bowling. He is recognized nationally and internationally as an author, speaker, and top coach of the pros. He has coached more than 100 pros, and many of the bowlers he's worked with—including David Ozio, Del Warren, Randy Pedersen, Steve Hoskins, and Kent Wagner—won their first titles after working with him.

In honor of his coaching expertise, Jowdy has been inducted into the Professional Bowling Association (PBA) Hall of Fame and the American Bowling Congress (ABC) Hall of Fame as well as the Texas Bowling Hall of Fame and the San Antonio Bowling Hall of Fame. He has worked with virtually every world-class bowler, including Donna Adamek, Mike Aulby, Parker Bohn III, Nikki Gianulias, Marshall Holman, Dave Husted, Tish Johnson, John Mazza, Amleto Monacelli, Betty Morris, Robin Romeo Mossontte, Mark Roth, Rick Steelsmith, Brian Voss, Lisa Wagner, Chris Warren, Pete Weber, and Danny Wiseman.

Jowdy is known for teaching the execution and skill of the game, and he has been called the master of teaching the free armswing. He teaches privately and conducts a seminar series, Bowling at the Highest Level. He's also a skilled and prolific writer. He has received numerous writing awards, including the most prestigious awards a bowling writer can receive: the Flowers for the Living Award, the Mort Luby Meritorious Award, and the DBA Humanitarian Award. A former president of the Bowling Writers Association of America, he continues to write a syndicated monthly column that is carried in more than 20 national publications, as well as instructional columns for *Bowling Digest* and *Bowling This Month*. Columbia Industries, for whom Jowdy serves as pro tour consultant, has established an annual college scholarship in his honor.

Jowdy lives in San Diego, California, with his wife, Brenda.